Archetypes in
Life, Literature, and Myth

Shelley Ni Tuama

The Center for Learning

Shelley Ni Tuama earned her B.A. from Bennington College and her M.A. from the University of Chicago Divinity School. She has taught high school English and college religion courses and tutored remedial students in English language skills.

The Publishing Team

Rose Schaffer, M.A., President/Chief Executive Officer
Bernadette Vetter, M.A., Vice President
Tammi McCune, M.A., Editor

Cover Design

Krina K. Walsh, B.S.I.D.

List of credits found on Acknowledgments Page beginning on 83.

ISBN 1-56077-487-8

Contents

Introduction

This unit is an introduction to archetypes designed for high school students in advanced placement and honors level English courses. In these twelve lessons, students will encounter a series of archetypal figures and patterns as they are played out in various contexts, including world literature, poetry, and myth. These lessons will also engage them in recognizing and responding to archetypal images within their own life experience.

Carl Gustav Jung, the ground-breaking psychoanalyst, introduced the idea of the archetype into public discourse. While much of his psychoanalytic theory and approach centers on dream analysis, these universal symbols have become the subject of literary analysis as well. The focus of this unit is to look closely at some examples of these archetypes, such as the Mother Goddess, the Sacred Marriage, and the Trickster, and to decipher their meanings as they surface in myth, literature, and contemporary life.

This material is accessible to advanced placement and honors high school students. Although sometimes appearing deceptively simple, these concepts run deep and require careful analysis to uncover their significance. This study will challenge students to apply their critical thinking skills, deepen their understanding of symbols, exercise their imaginations, and develop their creative writing abilities. It will also speak to them on a personal level as these students' stage of life is laden with expressions of archetypal motifs. By working through the lessons in this unit, students will identify and interpret patterns and figures central to their current experiences, such as the rite of passage known as initiation.

Young people face an increasingly disjointed and fragmented society. Studying some of the archetypal images that underlie the world they stand to inherit can reassure them that there *is* some integrity and order to be found after all. As teachers we try to lead our students to a deeper understanding of themselves and the world by directing them in the manner of the Benevolent Guide figure. However, they must ultimately make their own way and navigate this difficult passage into adulthood by themselves. May these insights shed light on their path which is certain to be filled with new forces to confront and unique trials to overcome as they cross over the threshold into maturity.

Teacher Notes

Using the Course Materials

This unit consists of teacher plans and student handouts for twelve lessons. These lessons are designed to challenge advanced placement and honors English literature students to think about symbols in a new way. More basic educational approaches to the subject of mythology and symbols are available through other Center for Learning texts.

The lessons are designed around archetypal themes and figures and most will require more than one class period to cover adequately. The unit is comprised of three core sections: the first four lessons serve as a general introduction to these concepts; the second four lessons explore various forms of a particular archetypal pattern known as initiation; and the last four lessons introduce additional archetypal figures.

The handouts are numbered for quick reference and are to be distributed to students. Keep in mind that suggested responses to the handout questions are only guidelines. Answers will vary unless otherwise indicated.

Encourage students to retain handouts for reference and review. There are numerous secondary references cited throughout the Notes to the Teacher sections for teachers to supplement their knowledge of this subject. A complete bibliography of these references is included at the end of the unit.

Teaching Approaches

This unit offers many different approaches to working through the material with students. Large and small group discussion, creative writing activities, and a variety of follow-up projects are provided. Teachers may adapt these activities as needed. A list of additional activities is given at the end of the unit. Reinforcement of these concepts will be needed as you go along; therefore, allow time for review.

Evaluation

Evaluation of students' command of this material may take several forms. Lesson handouts may be used as a means to check short-term comprehension. Follow-up activities including potential discussion or essay questions are provided throughout the unit to exercise students' critical thinking skills. There are also student directed projects and creative writing activities which can be used to evaluate progress. Several examples of timed-writings utilizing the themes covered are provided at the end of the unit.

It is The Center for Learning's goal to make materials easily accessible for teachers. With this goal in mind, we attempt to print all works covered in a curriculum unit, except those widely anthologized. We make a special effort to print works which may be difficult to obtain. Unfortunately, sometimes we are denied permission to print a work or are limited by its length.

Below is a list, by lesson, of works utilized in *Archetypes in Life, Literature, and Myth* that need to be secured by the teacher. We have attempted to list the most easily accessible publications of each work.

Lesson 2   Yeats, W.B. "Brown Penny." *The Collected Poems of W.B. Yeats.* New York: Macmillan Publishing Company, 1979.

Lesson 2–3   Angelou, Maya. "On the Pulse of Morning." New York: Random House, Inc., 1993.

Lesson 7   Anderson, Sherwood. "Sophistication." *Winesburg, Ohio.* New York: Viking Press, 1960.

                  Joyce, James. *Portrait of the Artist as a Young Man.* Paperback edition. New York: Penguin USA, 1977; pages 165–173.

Lesson 9   Faulkner, William. "The Bear." *Uncollected Stories of William Faulkner.* Joseph Blotner, ed. New York: Random House, 1979.

Lesson 10   Hawthorne, Nathaniel. "The Maypole of Merry Mount." *Norton Anthology of American Literature, Volume 1.* Third edition. New York: W.W. Norton and Company, 1989.

                  Jackson, Shirley. "The Lottery." *Literature, Structure, Sound, and Sense.* Orlando: Harcourt Brace, 1970.

Lesson 1
Describing Sign, Symbol, and Archetype

Objectives
- To introduce the Jungian concepts of sign, symbol, and archetype

- To identify the ways a classic archetype, the circle, serves as a collective image

Notes to the Teacher

Before students can identify and analyze archetypal patterns in literature and life, they must be introduced to the work of Carl Jung who established the concept of archetype. In this first lesson, students will become acquainted with Jung's theories, in particular his distinction between the three similar and often confused terms: sign, symbol, and archetype. Some of the materials in this lesson are derived from Carl Jung's own writing, "Approaching the Unconscious" from *Man and His Symbols*. This well-illustrated text geared for the general reading public is strongly recommended as a supplementary reference for the teacher (as well as the advanced student) undertaking this unit.

As a pioneer in the field of psychology, Jung's approach focuses on the psychoanalytic features of the archetype and directs many commentaries to dream analysis within individual case histories. This unit is concerned with analyzing archetypal patterns and figures as they emerge in life, literature, and myth. The psychological ramifications of these images and motifs are outside the scope of this study. While Jung publically recognized the expression of archetypal patterns in literary and artistic works and wrote articles in this vein, it has been left to the auspices of literary critics and history of religion scholars to explore this territory within world literature and cultural traditions. The academic study of comparative mythology falls somewhere between the disciplines of literature and religious studies in its attempt to unlock the meaning behind the written record of a culture's belief system. While this guide to archetypes is *not* a religion unit, valuable insights into the Jungian theory of archetypes can be found in many texts which fall into the categories of religious studies and myth. One introduction, "The Dimensions of Myth," can be found in the anthology *The World of Myth* compiled by English professor David Adams Leeming.

This literary analysis refers to the depth psychology of Sigmund Freud and especially Jung which is concerned with the dimensions of the collective unconscious. Freud and Jung believe its contents are shared by all humankind. The images which arise out of this collective unconscious are known as archetypes. These universal symbolic forms present themselves in dreams and myths of individuals and societies. Jung and his followers discerned that archetypes arise spontaneously in the mythic motifs of all cultures in such representations as the Mother Goddess, the Hero, the Trickster-God, initiation, sacrifice-death-regeneration, and so on. In this school of thought, sacred stories provide more than a form of explanation. For Jungians, these motifs are the formations of the transcendent human psyche. They are emanations of the collective unconscious that help shape our behavior in very real ways. They allow us even in modern day to live mythically.

The activities in this first lesson will encourage students to use their own common knowledge and acquired insight to uncover the distinctions between Jung's notions of sign, symbol, and archetype. They will look at a classic example of an archetype to see how it operates. Take enough time at this early point to determine that students have a firm grasp of these concepts, as they will form the foundation for the rest of the work in this unit.

Procedure

1. Ask students to write their own definitions of sign and symbol, and then have them put these to one side.

2. Give a brief overview of Carl Jung's work and its impact on twentieth century thought (see Notes to the Teacher).

3. Distribute **Handout 1**. Read through the synopsis of Jung's definitions with the students. Use the bottom of the worksheet to lead the students through an analysis of the two concepts sign and symbol. Identify the forms, features, and manifestations of each concept using the synopsis of Jung's definitions. Have students include their own examples of signs and symbols on their charts.

Suggested Responses:

Sign

Forms—*initials, word, or object image*

Features

> 1. *meaningless in itself; gains meaning through common usage or intention*
>
> 2. *designates the object it refers to*

Manifestations (Examples)—*abbreviations, insignia, trademarks, etc. (UN, NASA, Coke, Tylenol, police badge)*

Symbol

Forms—*term, name, or picture image*

Features

> 1. *contains conventional meaning via common usage, but also carries a special connotation*
>
> 2. *implies more than its commonly held meaning; contains an "unconscious" aspect one can't exactly pin down*

Manifestations (Examples)—*religious artifacts, dream images, political emblems (the cross, dream images of flying or falling down, dove, the American flag)*

4. Have students share their preliminary definitions of sign and symbol with the class. Compare their definitions with the Jungian description they have arrived at to see how the terms have been enlarged or clarified through analysis.

5. As a homework assignment, ask students to sift through magazines, newspapers and other handy printed materials to clip examples of signs and symbols and have them label each accordingly. Have them present these to each other in class and/or post them on a bulletin board.

6. Distribute **Handout 2**. Read through the synopsis of Jung's description of archetype and discuss the various ideas as a class. Ask students to think of examples of "the universal hero myth" (as noted in item 6) they have come across in their studies (Hercules, Theseus, Beowulf, etc.). Have students retain descriptive handouts as references for future lesson activities.

7. Explain to students that an archetype is a unique type of symbol, a kind of super-symbol that can take a number of forms: an abstract idea or a single entity, such as a circle or a wheel; a charismatic figure, such as a hero or a heroine; a pattern of behavior, such as a vision quest or an initiation ritual; a theme, such as death and rebirth or redemption; and even a number, like four which depicts the four corners of the earth or the four seasons of the year in Navaho art. Note that an archetype is always a symbol or symbolic pattern of some sort, but a symbol is not always an archetype.

The Continuum Dictionary of Religion definitions of archetype and symbol may help clarify this distinction further. (You may want to give these definitions to students for their reference):

archetype: A term used primarily in the analytical psychology of Carl Gustav Jung. Archetypes are instinctive patterns in the collective unconscious of humankind. Each individual shares, thus, through birth in a common heritage of experiential structures. Archetypes have through the course of history manifested themselves in the form of myths, tales, legends, pictoral representations, symbols (crosses, stars, mandala, etc.).

symbol: An object that stands for something more abstract or general. The cross, for example, is a symbol in Christianity representing Christ's suffering and death. Symbols usually presuppose a certain learning process in order to be fully understood. Through attachment to specific emotional experiences and models of thought, symbols acquire great importance in the creation of intense experiences and commonly have clear implications for action based on belief.[1]

[1] Michael Pye, ed., *The Continuum Dictionary of Religion*, (New York: Macmillan Press Ltd., 1994), 19, 259.

Note that the cross appears as an example of an archetype as well as an example of a symbol in these definitions. Inform students that some images can and do act in both capacities.

8. Distribute **Handout 3** to students and ask them to consider this classic example of an archetype—the circle—as it appears in the Oglala Sioux tribal religion of Black Elk.

9. Work with students to identify the ways this circular image acts as an archetype in this Native American tribal account.

Suggested Responses:

1. *Power of the World came to the tribe from a sacred hoop. The Power works in circles, thus all aspects of tribal life reflect this formation.*

2. *Sky, earth, and stars are round shaped.*

3. *Wind whirls in a circular shape.*

4. *Birds' nests are in circles.*

5. *The sun and the moon are round and rise and set in a circular fashion.*

6. *Seasons are circular—a cycle of continual change.*

7. *Human life is a cycle. Each person begins as a child, grows into an adult, and returns to childike ways as a dependent elderly person.*

8. *Tepee dwellings are round and are set in a circle.*

10. Ask students if the circle carries any symbolic meaning or archetypal power in their own lives or belief systems. Ask students to see if any of their own cultural or religious circular symbolism parallels the Oglala Sioux archetypal representations. For example, do they think of the calendar year as circular or linear? (Responses might include: Eucharist wafer, Advent wreath, wedding ring, yin/yang symbol, mandala, etc.)

Sign vs. Symbol

In *Man and His Symbols*, Carl Jung begins his chapter "Approaching the Unconscious" by making a distinction between a symbol and a sign. Read through the following synopsis with your teacher and fill in the forms and features areas in the chart below for each concept. Once you have identified Jung's basic tenets on your chart, you may fill in your own examples in the manifestations column.

Human beings use oral and written language to communicate meaning. Our vocabulary is filled with a variety of signifiers. We often use signs or images to communicate our intentions. These expressions called signs are not meaningful in themselves. Jung mentions several forms that such signs take, including abbreviations or acronymns, recognizable trademarks, the names of products, badges, and insignia. These signs carry meaning for a given society by their common usage and intention. Such things are not symbols. They are signs, and they do no more than signify the objects to which they refer.

On the other hand, Jung defines a symbol as "a term, a name, or even a picture that may be familiar in daily life, yet that possesses specific connotations in addition to its conventional and obvious meaning." This additional connotation attached to a symbol often eludes our conscious mind. The symbolic meaning exists for us but is not entirely realized. Jung mentions such objects as the wheel and the cross that are known all over the world yet that have a symbolic significance in certain contexts. In this way, a symbol implies something more than its apparent and immediate meaning. It has a larger "unconscious" aspect that can not be completely comprehended. We can seek to analyze a symbol, but we can never fully explain or define its import.[2]

	Forms	Features	Manifestations (Examples)
Sign		1.	
		2.	
Symbol		1.	
		2.	

[2] Carl Gustav Jung, ed., "Approaching the Unconscious," *Man and His Symbols* (New York: Doubleday and Company Inc., 1964), 20–21.

Synopsis of Jung's Description of Archetypes from
Man and His Symbols[3]

Read through the following synopsis of Carl Jung's description of archetypes.

1. Humankind produces images unconsciously in the form of dreams. The dream images of modern people correspond to the sacred story images and myths of primitive people. These "archaic remnants" are known also as "primordial images" or archetypes. Archetypes are, in essence, the stuff of dreams!

2. Archetypes come from a *tendency* all human beings have to form mythological images and motifs. Although this tendency shows up in conscious representations that vary in *detail* tremendously from person to person, culture to culture, and era to era, the *"basic pattern"* of the archetype remains the same. The archetype may manifest itself differently according to the context it appears in, but its essential form endures.

3. Archetypes are similar in nature to instincts, but unlike instinctual behavior they are not oriented in our physiology. They often reveal themselves to our consciousness by powerful symbolic images.

4. Archetypes have no known origin. They reproduce themselves in any time or place spontaneously.

5. Archetypal forms are dynamic. Archetypes give off a vitalizing force when people allow themselves to experience them—in Jung's words "to be brought under their spell."

6. Archetypes are collective; often a particular one is held in common by a social group. In this way, they are distinguished from personal complexes in that they create myths, religions, and philosophical systems that profoundly effect and characterize national identities and constitute historical legends. For example, the universal hero myth always refers to a powerful person or god-figure who vanquishes evil in the form of dragons, monsters, and so on and who liberates his people from destruction and death.

7. Archetypes appear deceptively simple on the surface, but are remarkably complex in substance. Jung decribes them as a "complex web of patterns." The longer one looks into them, the more intricate and labyrinthian they become.

8. Modern people are the first to identify these collective images as archetypes; primitive people seem to be more closely connected to their actual power and meaning. We have somehow lost the gift to fully experience them.

[3] Ibid., 67–103.

9. Archetypes are simultaneously both images and emotions. Only when these two aspects are present do they radiate. If there is only an image, then there is simply a word-picture (a sign) or a symbol of little consequence. However, when charged with emotion, the image holds "numinosity," or psychic energy. In Jung's words, "it becomes dynamic, and consequences of some kind must flow from it."

10. Archetype is a difficult concept to grasp because it defies a literal verbal description. Archetypes are not merely names of identifiable patterns or philosophical concepts; they are "pieces of life itself." Archetypal symbols are integrally connected to the living individual by the bridge of emotions.

11. According to Jung, "it is impossible to make an arbitrary or universal interpretation of an archetype." They need to be related to the whole-life experience and context of a given individual.

12. Each person must patiently try to uncover the significance an archetype conveys to him or her. Otherwise there is a real danger of finding merely "a jumble of mythological images which when strung together can refer to nothing or everything."

The Circle as Archetype

Read the following passage from *Black Elk Speaks* as an example of an archetype. In this account recorded by John Neidhardt, a tribal shaman known as Black Elk shares a vision. As a class, discuss the ways the circle acts as an archetype in the framework of Black Elk's tribe, the Oglala Sioux of the Northern Plains.

> You have noticed that everything an Indian does is in a circle, and that is because the Power of the World always works in circles, and everything tries to be round. In the old days when we were a strong and happy people, all our power came to us from the sacred hoop of the nation, and so long as the hoop was unbroken, the people flourished. . . . Everything the Power of the World does is done in a circle. The sky is round, and I have heard that the earth is round like a ball, and so are all the stars. The wind, in its greatest power, whirls. Birds make their nests in circles, for theirs is the same religion as ours. The sun comes forth and goes down again in a circle. The moon does the same, and both are round. Even the seasons form a great circle in their changing, and always come back again to where they were. The life of a man is a circle from childhood to childhood, and so it is in everything where power moves. Our teepees were round like the nests of the birds, and these were always set in a circle, the nation's hoop, a nest of many nests, where the Great Spirit meant for us to hatch our children.[4]

---

[4] Willis G. Regier, ed., *Masterpieces of American Indian Literature* (Lincoln: University of Nebraska Press, 1993), 557.

Lesson 2
Applying the Concepts Sign, Symbol, and Archetype

Objectives

- To examine a penny's ability to act as a sign or a symbol or to convey an archetypal pattern in different contexts

- To analyze symbolic images in poetry to determine how they operate as archetypes

Notes to the Teacher

This lesson serves as a continuation of Lesson 1 by directing students to apply their new understanding of signs, symbols, and archetypes within different contexts. Poetry is used as a vehicle to convey the significance of these forms as it speaks to the experiences common to all.

In an interview with Bill Moyers, published as *The Power of Myth* "The First Storytellers," the scholar Joseph Campbell reminds us that "myth must be kept alive." He says that the gifted artists and poets in modern culture "whose ears are open to the song of the universe" take on the responsibility of transmitting these mythic motifs to the rest of us.[1] This lesson uses the works of several world-class poets, W.B. Yeats, Walt Whitman, and Maya Angelou, to elucidate the concepts under discussion.

For the first activity, you will need to secure W.B. Yeats' brief poem "Brown Penny." An excerpt from Whitman's "When Lilacs Last in the Dooryard Bloom'd" has been reproduced on **Handout 4**. For the second activity, you will need to secure Angelou's inaugural poem, "On the Pulse of Morning." As a synthesizing activity, students are directed to compose an original poem using an archetypal image.

See the chapter "Archetypal Images and Themes" in P.W. Martin's *Experiment in Depth* for an overview of these concepts and a preview of several archetypal figures addressed in later lessons.

Procedure

1. When students are ready to move on and work with these concepts, divide the class into groups of three students. Give each group a penny indicating that this is a circular object with special significance in our culture. Direct students to interpret this object in three distinct ways: as a sign, as a symbol, and as a super-symbol having a larger, archetypal significance. Tell them to consider the obvious meaning and usage of the object, folklore or superstition attached to it, and any image depicted on it which carries meaning.

2. As students are interpreting the penny as a sign, symbol, and archetype, read aloud and/or distribute copies of Yeats' poem "Brown Penny." Tell students to consider this poem in their interpretations. Students will probably require prompting in the archetypal interpretation of the penny. If so, work through the suggested response as a class discussion. Note to students that the images depicted on coins of particular societies are often pictoral representations of archetypes significant to those cultures.

Suggested Responses:

Sign

a penny denotes 1 cent of US currency

Symbol

1. *A penny still denotes one cent, but it also implies an element of fortune or good luck in some instances: finding a lucky penny, keeping a jar of pennies in the kitchen, and a bride putting a penny in her shoe.*

2. *A penny can also carry an element of a wish being answered (folk belief of throwing a coin into a body of water), as in making a wish and tossing a coin into a wishing well.*

[1] Joseph Campbell, "The First Storytellers," *The Power of Myth*, (New York: Doubleday, 1988), 85.

Yeats' poem "Brown Penny" uses this image as a symbolic element of wishing for love. He plays on the symbolic circular images of the penny with the beloved's loops of hair and the moon as well as the assonance of the sounds "o" and "oo." At the same time, he personifies the penny as a confidant to the young man seeking guidance in love.

Archetype

The image on the front of a penny depicts the profile of Abraham Lincoln, the sixteenth president of the United States; the back depicts the Lincoln Memorial. The figure of Abraham Lincoln can be seen as an archetypal hero in our American history. His persona is invested with a special reverence as are his achievements, especially abolishing slavery (defeating this great evil), and he was assassinated (sacrificed) because of it.

3. Distribute **Handout 4**, the excerpt from Whitman's poem, "When Lilacs Last in the Dooryard Bloom'd." Tell students it was written as an elegy to President Lincoln and conveys the poet's emotional response to his death. Ask students to read it to discover the powerful significance this event had on Whitman's personal life and to hear him as a poet speaking for the nation as a whole—to feel the American people's response to this tragedy. Encourage students to look for the death and rebirth images in this poem.

Suggested Response:

Death images include drooping star, "Death's outlet," a coffin carrying a corpse travelling on a funeral train, dirges, etc. Rebirth images include "ever-returning spring," lilac bush with "heart-shaped leaves of rich green," miracle, "song of life," violets peep'd from general debris, apple blossoms, early lilies, etc.

Note: This particular response is cited, by Jungian scholar Joseph Henderson, as an example of "the drama of new birth through death," a universal archetypal motif found in world literature and myth.[2]

If necessary, explain to students that although the penny *itself* does not indicate an archetypal theme, the figure of slain President Lincoln represented on its face, as well as the shrinelike Lincoln Memorial featured on the flip side, do evoke this level of response in the collective American consciousness. Ask if any student having visited the Memorial in Washington D.C. would like to share their impressions of the atmosphere and emotions apparent at this site.

4. This is a follow-up activity as time allows (perhaps it can be given as an extended homework assignment). Distribute **Handout 5**. Have students work on an independent writing activity after reading and thinking about this news article, "Of Walt Whitman, who could hear America singing" by Paul Greenberg. Give students the option of choosing one of the following three essay topics to reflect upon the nature of the American dream:

1. Do you agree with Mr. Greenberg's statement, "the American dream is many dreams, each enhancing the other, point and counterpoint, like some great swelling chorus," or do you think the dreams of different Americans are in conflict—clashing against each other in disharmony?

2. Do you believe in an American Dream at all? If so, what is the status of it? Is it alive, or sleeping, or dead?

3. Do you believe that there was once a collective "American Dream," but it is no longer a reality? If so, what was the American Dream and how did we lose it?

Remind students that Jung believed archetypal symbols to be representative of a collective unconscious. Textbook writer Roger Schmidt characterizes them as "public dreams that bring humans into touch with the unconscious and transcendent depths of their experience."[3] These archetypes can become an expression of the feelings of a

[2] Joseph Henderson, "Ancient Myths and Modern Man," *Man and His Symbols*, ed. Carl Gustav Jung, (New York: Doubleday, 1964), 122–123.
[3] Roger Schmidt, "Sacred Stories," *Exploring Religion*, (Belmont, California: Wadsworth Publishing Company, 1988), 195.

nation as a whole. Similar to our nighttime dreams which can sometimes reflect our personal fears and waking concerns, these communal dreams shape our cultural values and direction.

5. Have students read "On the Pulse of Morning," Maya Angelou's inaugural poem. Then distribute **Handout 6** and have them answer the following questions independently.

Suggested Responses:

1. Each acts as an image that is charged with emotion. The Rock is crying for humanity to take a stand, the River is singing a song of unity, and the Tree is telling humanity to seek goodwill and the rebirth of the American Dream. The poet is trying to create a new morning for the American people with these images. She is celebrating the ushering in of a new president and administration with a theme of renewal conveyed by three key symbols that originally held dinosaur fossils. In the process of the poem she identifies herself with these images and then has them become synonymous with the country.

2. Renewal—new beginning to be faced with courage

3. Their common message is that even though history cannot be changed, we can learn from it. Also, each American has a right as well as a responsibility to reshape the American dream and to greet each other cordially as this new day opens.

6. Have each student write a brief poem taking one of these three entities, rock, river, or tree, as the central image. Remind students to think of the following elements as they are working on their poems:

1. Remark on the power inherent in this particular archetype for yourself. It may be an actual entity that you are familiar with such as a tree you climbed as a child, or a river you visited, or a favorite rock you collected. It also can be one from your imagination, reading, or dream life. It should, however, be a *personal* expression of your experience with this entity.

2. What adjectives come to mind to describe the entity? What metaphors and other figures of speech help create its vivid image? What sounds of language bring the entity to life? What feeling lies behind the entity for the speaker, or is the entity going to speak for itself?

7. Have each student select a single archetypal symbol to investigate on his or her own. Direct students to seek out references in literature, folk legends and songs, pictures, and movies. Suggestions of possible archetypes include:

Animal figures—dragon, snake, bull, frog, fish, bird

Geographical features—island, mountain, volcano, spring, desert, valley

Man-made objects—cup, jewel, spear, wall, ship, door, key, ball, wheel, road

Plant entities—flowers, wheat, seed, fruit

(For example, a hammer has found archetypal expression in the national symbol of the now defunct Soviet Union's a hammer and sickle, and it appears in the Peter, Paul, and Mary classic American folk song "If I Had a Hammer.")

When Lilacs Last in the Dooryard Bloom'd

When lilacs last in the dooryard bloom'd,
And the great star early droop'd in the western sky in the night,
I mourn'd, and yet shall mourn with ever-returning spring.

Ever-returning spring, trinity sure to me you bring,
Lilac blooming perennial and drooping star in the west,
And thought of him I love.

O powerful western fallen star!
O shades of night—O moody, tearful night!
O great star dissappear'd—O the black murk that hides the star!
O cruel hands that hold me powerless—O helpless soul of me!
O harsh surrounding cloud that will not free my soul.

In the doorway framing an old-farmhouse near the whitewash'd palings,
Stands the lilac-bush tall-growing with heart-shaped leaves of rich green,
With many a pointed blossom rising delicate, with the perfume strong I love,
With every leaf a miracle—and from this bush in the dooryard,
With delicate-color'd blossoms and heart-shaped leaves of rich green,
A sprig with its flower I break.

In the swamp in secluded recesses,
A shy and hidden bird is warbling a song.
Solitary thrush,
The hermit withdrawn to himself, avoiding the settlements,
Sings by himself a song.
Song of the bleeding throat,
Death's outlet song of life, (for well dear brother I know,
If thou wast not granted to sing thou woulds't surely die.)

Over the breast of spring, the land, amid cities,
Amid lanes and through old woods, where lately the violets peep'd from the
        ground, spotting the gray debris,
Amid the grass in the fields each side of the lanes, passing the endless grass,
Passing the yellow-spear'd wheat, every grain from its shroud in the dark-
        brown fields uprisen,
Passing the apple-tree blows of white and pink in the orchards,
Carrying a corpse to where it shall rest in the grave,
Night and day journeys a coffin.

Coffin that passes through lanes and streets,
Through day and night with the great cloud darkening the land,
With pomp of the inloop'd flags with the cities draped in black,
With the show of the States themselves as of crape-veiled women standing,
With processions long and winding and the flambeaus of the night,
With countless torches lit, with the silent sea of faces and the unbared
      heads,
With the waiting depot, the arriving coffin, and the somber faces,
With dirges through the night, with the thousand voices rising strong and
      solemn,
With all the mournful voices of the dirges pour'd around the coffin,
The dim-lit churches and the shuddering organs—where amid these you
      journey,
With the tolling tolling bells' perpetual clang,
Here, coffin that slowly passes,
I give you my sprig of lilac.

(Nor for you, for one alone,
Blossoms and branches green to coffins all I bring,
For fresh as the morning, thus would I chant a song for you O sane and
    sacred death.

All over bouquets of roses,
O death, I cover you over with roses and early lilies,
But mostly and now the lilac that blooms the first,
Copious I break, I break the sprigs from the bushes,
With loaded arms I come, pouring for you,
For you and the coffins all of you O death.)

                —*Walt Whitman*

Of Walt Whitman, who could hear America singing

Walt Whitman, who heard America singing, would be our national poet if this continental nation could contain only one national poet.

In his rugged grandeur, in his all-embracing enthusiasm for all things and futures American, in his infallible love and hopeless optimism, in his soaring vision and uncontainable spirit, in all his desperate acceptance, Walt Whitman remains as American as a poet can be. Indeed, he began his preface to the original, 1855 edition of "Leaves of Grass" with the word America.

That was the work in which he announced his great discovery: "The United States themselves are essentially the greatest poem."

Did ever a nation have such a celebrant, or need one to show it to itself? The poet's view of his country was both solitary and all-inclusive. The feelings he exuded in great rushes of words ("I too am not a bit tamed, I too am untranslatable,/I sound my barbaric yawp over the roofs of the world . . .") will not be foreign to the American seeing Old Glory in a foreign land, or attending a naturalization ceremony, or glimpsing the wilderness of the American interior, or descending into the teeming cities of these, yes, still united states, or looking anywhere in this whole swirling mass of a continental poem.

There was in Walt Whitman's compedious, encyclopedic, all-devouring, all-accepting love of life and his country a healthy measure of lust, too. He would be fired from his job as a clerk at the Department of Interior because of the "licentiousness" of his works.

It wouldn't be the first job that his ideas—or rather daring to express them— would cost him. Free-soil Democrat that he was, he would be bounced as editor of the Brooklyn Eagle in the 1840s for not hewing to the national party's pro-slavery line.

"A great people," a poet of the law would say, "does not go to its leaders for incantations or liturgies by which to propitiate fate or cajole victory; it goes to them to peer into the recesses of its own soul, to lay bare its deepest desires; it goes to them as it goes to its poets and seers."

So said Learned Hand, who did not think to add that a great people goes to its poets and seers as it goes to its leaders—not for careful, calculated, well-balanced nothings, but for that vision without which a people perish.

Who even today can read the words of the Declaration of Independence afresh, striving to recapture that moment when they were first proclaimed, and not tremble at the vision those words loosed, not only for Americans but for those Walt Whitman called the Americans of all nations, as in his proud assertion: "The Americans of all nations at any time upon the Earth probably the fullest poetical nature."

By which the poet surely did not mean a gift for rhyme or even free verse, but a gift for freedom, for tolerance, for the fullest and ever expanding range of individualities.

In 1776, the American truth found its words, and was proclaimed with a flourish, not only for Americans, but for all, created equal and endowed by their Creator with certain rights. That theory remains as revolutionary today as it was 219 years ago, and it can still change the world.

Where is that broad, sweeping Whitmanesque spirit today? It is not easy to discern behind the petty sniping, the partisan games, the prudential calculations that have replaced the old faith in the providential, that once-sure sense of a dream shared.

Reactionaries and radicals this country has always had. Is not America itself a reaction against the old world? America has had her liberals and conservatives, too, but strange, new oxymoronic mutants begin to dominate the American conversation: the reactionary liberal and the reactionary conservative. Contradictory, bicephalic, blinkered, each rushes headlong to offer its own simple, narrow answers to questions that are neither simple nor narrow, as if they were prescribing not for a great, tumultuous nation but some lifeless schematic drawing.

The reactionary liberal—more reactionary than truly liberal—rushes to preserve every ruin of a statist past, however great a failure so many have proven. The reactionary conservative—more reactionary than truly conservative—would indiscriminately sweep aside every vestige of the recent past, rather than seek out and conserve what experience recommends.

Theory is now in the saddle and rides experience—the reverse of the pattern that only slowly and gradually produced the great Declaration of 1776, for America had grown independent long before she declared herself to be. This bold new experiment called America is also a cautious one. The elements in this Whitmanesque stew are so mixed, and the result still so distinctive, that it makes descriptions like liberal and conservative largely irrelevant.

A new dynamism can be felt in the American dialogue these days, but it must unite and liberate and elevate, like Walt Whitman's best, if it is transform drift into direction, the old malaise into a new sense of independence. Where now is the sweep, the grandeur, the Whitmanesque appeal of American ideas and deeds? Where it has always been—in the people themselves. Not the masses or classes, the The People, as in We the People, united but individual, even idiosyncratic.

Walt Whitman had a vision for himself, but it was not a vision that would interfere with any other American's. He understood that the American poem is sung by many poets, and that the American dream is many dreams, each enhancing the other, point and counterpoint, like some great swelling chorus.

Paul Berman, searching Brooklyn for the house in which Whitman once lived, reported in the New Yorker not long ago that he had found it: 99 Reyerson St. He also reported what happened when he went there:

"I climbed the red stoop and pressed a buzzer at random. The door opened and two brothers peered out. I introduced myself and told them the exciting antiquarian news that in their own home the greatest of American poets had once lived-more than a century ago. Then one of them—a Mr. Clifford Richardson, a highly trained electrician (as I later learned) with a sideline as 'Watongo,' reggae singer—cocked his head and asked, in the accent of St. Kitts, 'How do you know there isn't a great poet living here now?'"

There. There is the spirit of Walt Whitman's America, and it is still sings forth.[1]

[1]Paul Greenberg, "Of Walt Whitman, Who Could Hear America Singing," *The Plain Dealer*, July 5, 1995.

Rock, River, and Tree

Read "On the Pulse of Morning" by Maya Angelou and answer the questions below.

1. How can the three main images, a Rock, a River, and a Tree, be viewed as archetypes in "On the Pulse of Morning" by Maya Angelou? Explain using your knowledge of archetype.

2. What theme(s) runs through this poem?

3. Each of the three personified images communicates differently: The Rock cries, the River sings, and the Tree speaks. Which method, if any, is most effective? What is their common message?

4. What is the poet expressing by ending with the line "Good Morning"?

5. Do these images, a Rock, a River, and a Tree bring to mind any archetypal expressions in your own life? Do they speak to *you* on an archetypal level?

Lesson 3
The Importance of Studying Archetypes

Objectives
- To identify how archetypes function in our lives

- To examine two examples of archetypes as they surface in contemporary culture

Notes to the Teacher
Beyond the initial observation that archetypes are an interesting study in themselves, students may require some additional understanding as to why this type of analysis is important. This lesson will give them a rationale to help them understand the pertinence of this study to modern life. As students have already undoubtedly discovered, images of symbols and archetypes abound in literature. Mythic motifs form a myriad of themes, characters, and plot lines in the great artistic masterworks of all mediums, literary, visual, and musical. They also appear in popular culture in many forms, including films, songs, comic books, and news articles. One obvious reason to look into archetypes and archetypal patterns is to better understand such allusions in artistic as well as popular culture.

But perhaps there are even more profound reasons to engage in this study than simply providing students with another way to critique literary works and contemporary culture. Joseph Campbell, scholar of comparative mythology, comments on this subject in several writings, including one of his most helpful texts, *Hero With a Thousand Faces*, which discusses the place of myth in the modern world. (This text is a strongly recommended supplementary reference and will be invaluable in the upcoming lessons dealing with the hero and initiation rituals.) In the last chapter, "Myth and Society," Campbell outlines the ways myth has been interpreted in the past and looks at how myth continues to serve humankind in the present.

In writing about the function of mythology, Campbell denotes four distinct ways that sacred stories serve humankind: mystical, cosmo- logical, sociological, and psychological functions. These are found in his survey of world mythology, *Masks of God, Volume 3, Occidental Mythology*.

1. To convey a mystical experience in which the sacred is manifested or somehow recognized

2. To fulfill the human desire to explain how the cosmos came into being and how human life evolved; also, to provide a sense of security that there is an order to our existence

3. To give us a social sensibility—to construct our social identity and to govern our behavior

4. To help the individual understand who he or she is by guiding them through life's rites of passage, such as birth, puberty, marriage, old age, and death—to construct our personal identity[1]

Procedure
1. Tell students that since they have become familiar with the description of an archetype and have delved into some examples, they are ready to see how archetypes function. Direct them to look over the examples of archetypes from Lessons 1 and 2 to identify what function they serve, or to determine their purpose and uncover what service they provide to the individual and/or society.

2. Distribute **Handout 7**. Have students complete the archetype and function sections. These may be completed as a whole class exercise (perhaps with the teacher using the overhead or board) or independently. (Note that an interesting distiction arises between the context of the Whitman and the Angelou poem. They both celebrate American presidents at different phases, but one is an ode to a dead leader and the other is an inspiration to a leader just rising to

---

[1] Joseph Campbell, *Masks of God, Volume 3, Occidental Mythology*, (New York: Penguin Books, 1976), 519–522.

power.) Students may want to include other archetypal referents from their past literary reading or experience.

Suggested Responses: (see chart below)

3. Give students the four functions of myth or sacred stories established by Joseph Campbell (See Notes to the Teacher).

4. Have students refer back to **Handout 7** and enter in the Campbell's four types section the number(s) of these functions that may correspond to the student's own descriptive entry. Inform students that while Campbell's categories were describing the functions of "myth," these four functions can be applied to the manner in which archetypes serve humankind. Note that it is possible and probable to have more than one function working in a given archetypal reference.

Suggested Responses:

Black Elk 1, 2, 3, 4

Whitman's poem 3, 4

Angelou's poem 3, 4

5. Distribute **Handout 8**, the *Newsday* article "Birth of the Bomb" by Fred Bruning. Ask students to look at this illustration of a twentieth century cataclysmic incident in American and world history. Have them read the article and highlight the archetypal reference within this incident.

Suggested Response:

J. Robert Oppenheimer's famous words upon viewing the blast, quoted from a passage of sacred Hindu scripture: "I am become Death, the shatterer of worlds."

Suggested Responses, Handout 7:

Source	Archetype	Function(s) for Individual or Society
Black Elk Speaks	*circle image*	• *Describes the origins of the world and the tribe* • *Provides a guiding principle and structure to tribal life* • *Gives the people a sense of order to the natural world*
"When Lilacs Last in the Dooryard Bloom'd" by Walt Whitman	*1. President Lincoln as hero figure* *2. Death-rebirth theme*	• *Provides a grieving nation with a way to think about the president's death—making sense out of a senseless tragedy* • *Allows an outlet to great personal and national grief* • *Conveys a sense of hope in a time of darkness and distress*
"On the Pulse of Morning" by Maya Angelou	*Rock, River, and Tree*	• *Give American citizens a place to stand, rest, and draw strength; reinforces their right to be here* • *Challenges Americans to give birth to a new dream and to embrace the best in each other* • *Seeks to inspire a new president and administration taking office*

18

6. Lead a discussion on this archetypal reference. Inform students that Oppenheimer's quote is a reference to a sacred Hindu text, the *Bhagavad Gita*, in which Krishna reveals himself as the incarnation of the supreme lord by blazing like a thousand suns. Oppenheimer recalled the verse describing Krishna in his destructive mode as "shatterer of worlds." Krishna was identifying himself with the dual nature of glory and destruction ascribed to supreme male deity in the Hindu pantheon. Have students research this Krishna figure and/or provide mythic background for them. (Refer to the section on Hinduism of a text such as Huston Smith's *The World's Religions*.)

    In your discussion, underline the significance of this comment by Oppenheimer by asking students to reflect on the following:

    Of all the possible responses he could have made, why did Oppenheimer choose this archetypal image, "Death" personified, to describe the event? Is it an appropriate comment in the opinion of the students? What is he saying about this new force humankind has discovered? (Note: Scholar Wendy Doniger O'Flaherty believes it is significant that Oppenheimer chose a myth *outside* his own culture to describe this experience.) Why would a person cite a reference from another tradition at such a moment? Would a reference from the Judeo-Christian tradition speak to the experience just as well? If so, can students think of any that might be as powerful and descriptive as the Hindu reference?

7. Continue the discussion by asking students to surmise which of Campbell's functions is being enacted here.

    Suggested Response:

    Possibly 4, a rite-of-passage for the world community as they enter the nuclear age, but this is stretching it. None of the functions fully corresponds to this unique experience.

8. Suggest to students that they compose their own function 5 to describe the function being fulfilled in Oppenheimer's usage of the archetype.

Possible Response:

Such archetypal images serve to mark critical moments in human history. They provide symbolic referents which help us place unique events in some established context. Using mythological symbolism gives humankind a way to think about new realities.

9. Extended homework assignment: Ask students to look through the editorial pages of local newspapers or accessible large city newspaper and/or news magazines for other examples of archetypal referents as they appear in current events.

Optional Activities

1. Distribute **Handout 9**, a newspaper article excerpt entitled "Disney's version of Pocahontas unlike the historical" by Joan Connell. Ask students to read and highlight the section that refers to the archetypal aspect of the legend of Pocahontas.

Suggested Responses:

"Pocahontas is laden with the need of 19th- and 20th-century Americans to have a story of the primal mother. . . . That mother, the representative of nature, can reconnect us with nature and teach us the language we have forgotten."

(Inform students that this "primal mother" archetype will be the focus of the next lesson.) At this point, you may want students to break into groups to discuss the function of the Pocahontas legend for our society. Does it correspond to any of Campbell's functions? How do we potentially benefit from the retelling of this story?

2. You may assign students a project of researching the historical record of Pocahontas and/or critically viewing the Disney film *Pocahontas*. Have them compare and contrast the impact of each version. A possible topic for debate and/or essay may ask students to think about Disney productions as a conveyer of American mythology. Does the company do our society a service producing these films? Is the power and emotion of the archetype coming through according to Jung's description? Is the company merely providing entertainment? Do such films as *Pocahontas* fulfill any of the functions covered in this lesson?

Functions of Archetypes

Source	Archetype	Function(s) for Individual and/or Society	Functions
Black Elk Speaks			
"When Lilacs Last in the Dooryard Bloom'd" by Walt Whitman			
"On the Pulse of Morning" by Maya Angelou			
(Other)			

Birth of the Bomb

A storm boiled in the desert. Winds hit 30 mph and rain flogged the barren acreage of the government's Alamogordo Bombing Range. Lightning splintered the sky.

At 2:30 a.m., a floodlamp blew out briefly and the 100-foot tower it illuminated blended into the inky New Mexico horizon.

As though in a final operatic flourish, nature was heralding its power and prerogatives. Man's turn would come next.

Bad weather retreated and scientists counted toward a 5:30 a.m. zero-hour.

Attention focused on the tower, again bathed in light. At the top was a metal shack and in the shed, the bulbous form known as "the gadget"—a strangely benign tag for a weapon so formidable that some wondered if the test soon to take place would consume the compound, or the city of Los Alamos about 150 miles away, or the state of New Mexico, or whether detonation of the first atomic bomb simply would set the atmosphere on fire and smother the world.

Describing the A-bomb's debut, a reporter for The New York Times—the only journalist invited—wrote, "On that moment hung eternity."

But J. Robert Oppenheimer, the brilliant, meditative physicist who helped build the bomb, said later he was reminded of a passage from sacred Hindu scripture. As the A-bomb's incandescent mushroom cloud imposed its false and frightening sunrise on the site code-named Trinity, Oppenheimer pondered a sobering verse from the Bhagavad-Gita: "I am become Death, the shatterer of worlds."

Fifty years ago today, the Atomic Age began with a bang equal to 17,000 tons of TNT. Science had harnessed the energy of the universe and at the same time nudged the planet toward extinction—a cruel dichotomy that haunted people then as now.

But a path had been chosen.

Only three weeks after Trinity, a B-29 named the Enola Gay dropped an A-bomb fueled by uranimum on the Japanese industrial city of Hiroshima. Dubbed "Little Boy," the bomb was a wrathful intruder of unprecedented fury.

A great blast of superheated air toppled much of the city and, in an instant, killed 80,000 residents—many of them literally vaporized as though in some dreadful science-fiction episode.

Before Japanese leaders could come to grips with the Aug. 6 attack, the United States dropped a plutonium-based bomb on Nagasaki. Forty thousand people died when the device known as "Fat Man" detonated just after 11 a.m. Aug. 9. Scores more would perish from radiation exposure. Burned, disfigured and in excruciating pain, survivors were not necessarily the most fortunate.

Though heartbreaking, the devastation meant U.S. researchers at the nuclear warfare group known as the Manhattan Project had brought years of intense work to successful conclusion.

In the view of many, thousands of American—and Japanese—lives were saved in the process. The bomb brought a swift close to the war in the Pacific—Japan surrendered Aug. 15—avoiding need for a U.S. invasion to finally rout a fierce but doomed enemy. Even conservative estimates foresaw weeks of savage fighting and staggering casualities, a formidable prospect for Americans already exhausted from the war in Europe.

Fallout from the A-bomb was not limited to the spread of radioactive particles.

There was a profound cultural, political and emotional impact, too, and humanity has struggled for a half-century to cope with the consequences. Art, literature and political conversation still shows signs of a kind of post-bomb jitteriness.

Contends former U.S. Interior Secretary Stewart Udall, now a lawyer who represents American victims of radiation poisoning: "No event of this century has left a deeper imprint on human consciousness."

If anything, that psychic bloom may be growing more vivid.

President Harry S Truman's decision to drop the A-bomb remains a matter of debate so passionate in the United States that it sometimes threatens to achieve critical mass. Postal authorities had to yank a mushroom cloud stamp after complaints that the image was bloodthirsty, and the Smithsonian Institution in Washington revised a Hiroshima exhibit because veterans branded it soft on the Japanese.

When a scaled-back show opened at the Smithsonian's National Air and Space Museum last month—minus the material opponents found infuriating—anti-bomb demonstrators poured blood and ashes on the Enola Gay, centerpiece of the exhibit.

Japan is at odds with itself, too.

Harsh memories accompany the 50th anniversary as well as a wrenching discussion over how, or if, to apologize for conduct during World War II. Surveys show the Japanese public favors a strong statement of remorse but—in an odd parallel to the Smithsonian affair—many veterans and their legislative support-ers say an apology should emanate from Washington, not Tokyo.

Japan's ruling coalition finally approved a compromise resolution expressing regret for inflicting "unbearable pain to people abroad, particularly in Asian countries," but the statement satisfied few Japanese and did little to settle the controversy.

Internal feuding aside, Japan generally has been a model of discipline and determination since the war. A sense of tranquility is likely to mark anniversary observations in a country that has vaulted from the ignominy of defeat to one of the world's premier manufacturing and financial powers—a stunning and speedy postwar comeback that few could have envisioned.

But while Japan's wounds mainly have healed, baffling moral questions about nuclear warfare—and the bombings of 1945—persist. From the outset, some critics argued that Truman and his advisers opted for a nuclear strike too hastily—the president scribbled a go-ahead in pencil immediately upon learning results of the Trinity test, an eye-witness told Newsday—and some analysts continue to argue today that the United States acted precipitously.

Many Americans head for meltdown when U.S. motives are challenged. Burr Bennett, a World War II veteran who opposed the original Smithsonian Insti-tution exhibit as head of a group called the Committee for the Restoration and Proper Display of the Enola Gay, resents what he says is a move "toward making the U.S. the culprit."

The atomic bomb "was a primary catalyst of the Cold War," Alperovitz said last year in an article for the publication Foreign Policy. But like many in the decision-making loop, Truman may have been a captive of history. "I don't see Harry Truman as any better or worse than any of us," Alperovitz told Newsday.

To Ed Hedemann of the New York-based peace group Enola Gay Action Committee, avoiding issues raised by Hiroshima could be hazardous to the health of the world.

Ten nations have atomic weapons or could build them quickly—the United States, Britian, France, China, Russia, India, Israel, North Korea, Pakistan, South Africa—and there is concern that additional members of the so-called "nuclear club" soon might be inducted.[2]

[2]Fred Bruning, "The Birth of the Bomb," *The News Herald,* July 16, 1995.

Disney's Version of Pocahontas Unlike the Historical

When Disney producer James Pentecost sought advice about how to portray the cartoon version of the flesh-and-blood Pocahontas, anthropologist Helen Rountree figured he wouldn't be interested in what she had to say.

"For starters, Pocahontas was naked and bald when she first encountered John Smith. You wouldn't want to put that in your film, would you?" Rountree tartly told Pentecost in 1992 when the project was still in the planning stages.

She explained that shaven-headed, prepubescent girls of Pocahontas' tribe generally went about unclothed. One of the few historically reliable accounts of Pocahontas describes her turning stark-naked cartwheels around the settlers' stockade, provoking the men inside.

It comes as no surprise to Rountree, who teaches at Old Dominion University in Norfolk, Va., that once Hollywood had its way with Pocahontas, the wild child of the Chesapeake would be transformed into a buckskin-clad Barbie—doe-eyed, docile and utterly romantic.

Disney's animated morality tale may entirely bypass the facts of history, but few parents would object to its message that nature is good, greed is bad and the impulse to make peace is a paramount virtue.

Yet as the legend of Pocahontas and John Smith resurfaces in popular culture as a politically correct, eco-friendly romance, it's clear that this fractured fairy tale of the first encounter between English settlers and tribal people reveals much more about the desires, virtues and values of the present than it does about the past.

"Most of the natives of Virginia claim to be descendants of Pocahontas: there's a reason for that," said literary critic Diane Krumrey, who has done extensive research at Princeton University on the many ways the Pocahontas story has been told.

"Americans need to retell the story of the first contact between English settlers and American Indians to make it a loving, interactive and mutually satisfying encounter," she said, "to knit themselves into the landscape with a love story that would produce a true American progeny."

The legend of Pocahontas also was fed over the centuries by French philosopher Jean-Jacques Rousseau, who popularized the idea of the "noble savage" as a source of wisdom that civilization has obliterated.

"Pocahontas is laden with the need of 19th– and 20th–century Americans to have a story of the primal mother," Krumrey says. "Pocahontas and Sacajawea [the Indian woman who guided Lewis and Clark on their westward exploration] are the only two 'savage mothers' in our cultural history. That mother, the representative of nature, can reconnect us with nature and teach us the language we have forgotten."

In some ways the real-life Pocahontas—who ultimately was captured by the English, married off to a colonist, baptized an Anglican, renamed Rebecca, dressed in gowns and presented to London society as a "civilized savage"—was as much of a cultural artifact as the legends that have grown up around her.

There is no real evidence, for instance, that Pocahontas saved John Smith from the wrath of her father. Most historians believe Smith fabricated the tale long after Pocahontas' death to capitalize on her fame.

And though John Rolfe, the English widower who ultimately married Pocahontas and fathered her child, publicly professed his enduring love for the Indian princess, Rountree and Krumrey say theirs was essentially a marriage of political convenience, designed to usher in a period of peace.

"She became a real political volleyball," Krumrey says of the historical Pocahontas, who died of smallpox at the age of 23. But more manipulation came later, as a young woman whose tribal culture had groomed her for greatness was reduced—in legends and now on film—to the sexual stereotype of a romantic heroine.

"Pocahontas became the paradigm of the perfect American woman—on the frontier or in the woods," Krumrey said. "Silent, in touch with nature, frail enough to be beautiful, but strong when we need her to be."

Paula Gunn Allen, a member of the Pueblo Laguna Sioux tribe and professor of literature at the University of California at Los Angeles, sees some advantages to Disney's retelling of the Pocahontas tale. But she, too, is troubled that Hollywood's sexual stereotyping eclipses much of the power women held in native cultures.

"At least the little ones will learn that this group of people had an effect on colonial life," said Allen, author of several books on the spirituality of tribal women.

Regardless of whether Pocahontas actually saved Smith, Allen said the legend ignores an important aspect of the motivation of Powhatan, Pocahontas' father.

"The story of how Pocahontas saved Smith's life completely ignores the fact that Powhatan wasn't indulging his sweet little daughter because she was pretty and in love," she said. "He had to [spare Smith's life] because women in tribal culture had the power over life and death."

Allen's idea of a politically correct animated feature on Pocahontas is significantly different from Disney's.

"I would set the movie in the village and I'd portray the settlers as they actually were—little, bitty white guys, filthy, because they never bathed, continually scratching themselves because of the lice they carried," she says.

"The Indians, who bathed even their children every morning in cold water, would reach out a helping hand to these derelict, disease-ridden and homeless boat people."

Allen's imagined film would go further than Disney's, which ends as Pocahontas and Smith are parted, to face separately an uncertain future. She would examine the year Pocahontas spent locked in a dungeon in the English stockade, then look critically at the life she lived in London.

"In the end, I wonder if she ended up a happy Christian, or whether she simply suffered from the 'Stockholm syndrome,' identifying with her captors," Allen said.

"It's unclear whether she ever really wanted to be baptized. She is silent on this, because she wasn't writing the history of her own life."[3]

---

[3]Joan Connell, "Disney's version of Pocahontas unlike the historical," *Religion News Service.*

Lesson 4
Manifestations of the Mother Goddess

Objectives

*   To introduce the archetype of the Mother Goddess

*   To identify the symbolic manifestations of the Mother Goddess

*   To write a modern profile of a goddess character

Notes to the Teacher

In this lesson students will be asked to draw on their knowledge of the major goddesses of the Greek pantheon to arrive at an understanding of the archetypal Mother Goddess figure. You may feel it necessary to provide them with a review of these major goddesses and their character traits before undertaking these activities. There are many fine anthologies for student review. One is the classic by Jean Hamilton, *Mythology*. Another more detailed analysis can be found in Robert Graves' two volume study, *The Greek Gods*.

There was a time when the Goddess was worshipped as the Great Mother throughout the ancient world. In these early cultures, the same female principle of Great Mother Goddess was revered, even though she took different names according to the local culture. By the time classical Greek civilization reached its golden hour, the archetypal Mother Goddess had been divided into "departmental goddesses," as scholar Jane Harrison calls them. These six female deities, Hera, Athena, Aphrodite, Persephone, Artemis, and Demeter, took on different aspects of the Great Mother Goddess in weakened forms.

This collection of goddesses is referred to as "the Great Mother Power" by Jennifer Barker Woolger and Roger Woolger in their text, *The Goddess Within*, a highly recommended background text for the teacher. "The Great Mother Power" was the regenerative force in all life forms and exemplified fertility. The Woolgers construct a Goddess Wheel (**Handout 2**) as a visual reinforcement for their analysis. You may wish to introduce students to this visual with the Woolger's comment:

> The Wheel is designed like a flower. The six goddesses, like petals, radiate from the Great Mother at the Center, who symbolizes the transcendent unity of all the goddesses belonging to a broader, transpersonal level of being that we call archetypal or universal.[1]

By beginning the work on archetypal figures using material that students are familiar with, such as these six goddesses from classical Greek mythology, students will build on earlier learning and gain confidence for the more complex archetypal figures to be encountered in later lessons.

The second part of lesson 4 focuses briefly on distinguishing the positive and negative personality traits that go into forming the full picture of the Great Mother Goddess. It is essential to point out to students right from the beginning that there is a definite difference between the *archetype* of the Great Mother Goddess and the *reality* of a person's own birth mother. Remind the class that as an archetype this figure is a composite pattern which appears across many cultures in dreams, myths, and sacred stories. While she may share some characteristics associated with our biological mothers, such as nurturing, caring, and compassion, the Great Mother Goddess is a symbolic entity.

The true Goddess archetype consists of both the positive aspects and the negative aspects, or dark side. This Terrible Mother aspect is lost for the most part in the minimized versions of the Great Mother Goddess that have come down to us. In the Greek pantheon only the goddess Persephone in her role as Queen of the Underworld hints at this frightening visage. One example of this aspect can be found in the figure of Medusa, the archetypal personification of death. Another example of this dark side is clearly evident in the Hindu goddess figure, Kali, with her representation of death, night, and the powers of destruction. This Terrible

[1] Jennifer Barker Woolger and Roger Woolger, *The Goddess Within: A Guide to Eternal Myths that Shape Women's Lives*, (New York: Fawcett Columbine, 1989), 42.

Mother is the other half of the All-Loving Mother persona of the Goddess. When integrated into the Great Mother Goddess, both sides combine to produce the primal mystery exhibited by her awesome powers of birth-death-rebirth.

Procedure

1. The Pocahontas follow-up activity at the end of Lesson 3 can be used as a transition into this lesson. Tell students that in Lessons 1–3 they became familiar with the term archetype and some ways which archetypes function in our society. Now they are ready to tackle examples of specific archetypal *figures* as they appear in world literature and myths. The first figure under consideration is perhaps the most prevalent figure of all. She is known by one label as the Great Mother Goddess.

2. Give students background information on the matriarchial cults of the Goddess. Stress the fact that even though this Goddess figure was assigned different names and took on different dimensions in cultures of the ancient world, the dynamic image or archetype behind these entities is the *same*: the Great Mother. The early stories in Greek mythology referred to this entity as Gaia, the Earth Mother (sometimes Rhea). Review the six major goddesses from classical Greek mythology with the students (See Notes to the Teacher).

3. Distribute **Handout 10**. Ask students to classify the six goddesses according to the characteristics inside the circle and write the goddesses' names beside each item. (Note that some goddesses fall into two characteristics in the sphere.)

   Suggested Responses:

   Hera—Queen of heaven; Athena—Giver of Wisdom and Protectress; Aphrodite—Goddess of Love; Persephone—Goddess of death; Artemis—Lady of Beasts; Demeter—Mother of All and Lady of Plants.

4. A possible follow-up activity would involve students researching Mother Goddess figures from different ancient world cultures.

   Possible examples to research:

   > *Egypt—Isis*
   > *Sumer—Inanna*
   > *Crete—Atana*
   > *Babylon—Ishtar*
   > *Greece—Gaia*
   > *Asia Minor—Cybele*
   > *Canaan—Astarte*
   > *Hebrew—Asherah*

   Have them indicate which jurisdiction their assigned goddess falls within using the categories on **Handout 10** as well as the mythological story and features which surround their assigned figure.

5. Distribute **Handout 11**, page 1. Ask students to list the six major Greek goddesses and to identify the psychological dynamic behind each of them. In other words, have them distinguish a domain that the individual goddess rules over and concerns that may be involved in that domain.

Suggested Responses:

Goddess	Domain	Concerns
Hera	*Power– Politics*	*Marriage, partnership, tradition, morality*
Athena	*Civilization– Wisdom*	*Education, culture, war, creative arts, and intellectual pursuits*
Aphrodite	*Love–Eros*	*Sexuality, romance, beauty, passion*
Persephone	*Underworld– Death*	*Psychic powers, clairvoyance, visions, dreams, death, and transformations*
Artemis	*Nature– Animal Husbandry*	*Hunting, wilderness, ecology, adventures*
Demeter	*Motherhood– Agriculture*	*Fertility of land and body, nurturance, generation, childbearing, mothering*

6. After they complete the chart, ask students to identify the symbols associated with each goddess figure and note them on the chart for reference. Tell students these symbolic representations sometimes appear in poetry, songs, art, and films to indicate the Goddess archetype or to suggest her power and/or influence is present.

Suggested Responses:

Hera: *crown, peacock*

Persephone: *narcissus, pomegranate, bat*

Athena: *helmet, weaving, owl, olive tree*

Artemis: *moon, wild beasts, especially the bear*

Aphrodite: *sea-foam, shell, dove, myrtle*

Demeter: *fruits of the harvest, corn*

7. Beyond these specific emblems, the ancient Great Mother Goddess figure had several key forms that manifested her overall presence. Students may have encountered some of them in their research into the Mother Goddesses of antiquity in the follow-up activity to procedure 4. These manifestations may be noted at this time. You may wish to have students speculate on the meaning behind each symbolic form:

Key Form of Mother Goddess	Meaning
Tree of life or sacred pillar	Symbol of regeneration
Cavern	Symbolic of the womb
Animals, such as snake	Symbolic of dark powers—regeneration
Golden butterfly or double-edged axe (labrys)	Symbol of rebirth, mystery of the labyrinth
Fish	Symbol of rebirth
Corn	Symbol of fertile growth—abundance

8. Optional activity: Ask students to identify national and international female figures and celebrities that exemplify these Goddess traits. Include fictional and film characters in the list.

9. Distribute **Handout 11**, page 2 as a review or as an evaluation activity. Have students use the information gathered in the columns in **Handout 11**, page 1 to fill in the Goddess Wheel circles as designated.

10. Most likely students will have focused on the positive traits associated with each goddess figure. It is important to note that this is only *half* the picture (refer to Notes to the Teacher). Using Persephone (or one of the other underworld goddess figures) as a prototype, point out that there is another side of the Goddess's personality.

Indicate that the Underworld and the frightening experiences, monsters, and other forces encountered there are symbolic of that part of the human psyche known as the *unconscious*. These myths showing the dark side of the Mother Goddess with destructive powers are symbolic of an individual's personal confrontation with this side of himself or herself. (This experience will be clarified in the upcoming lessons on the hero's initiation.)

11. Have students reflect on the myth of Persephone and Demeter as more than a story to explain the origins of the seasonal agricultural cycle. Ask them to look at this myth as a description of an initiation into womanhood. By experiencing a descent into the underworld and reemerging to rejuvenate the world, these two goddesses—along with a third, Hecate, who surfaces in this myth—merge to form a complete picture of the Mother Goddess. This triple-figure goddess, maiden-mother-crone—which corresponds to the three moon phases, waxing-full-waning—achieves a unity. Each aspect of the triple Goddess represents a specific stage of life: maidenhood, motherhood, and old age. Even though each phase of life the Goddess figure experiences is characterized by loss, a new understanding of life is also gained.[2]

[2] Ibid, 283–284.

Lead a discussion on the losses and gains involved in each stage of life suggested by the myth.

Suggested Responses:

Goddess	Loss	Gain
Persephone	*loss of innocence, maidenhood*	*gains a name or new identity (previously she is called "Kore" = maiden) and status as a ruler/wife*
Demeter	*loss of child–daughter*	*gains a new perspective on life; extends her sphere of interests to include others*
Hecate	*loss of childbearing potential and some physical vitality*	*gains a new stature as wise woman and becomes a resource for other women to turn to*

12. Ask students to translate each of the three goddesses stages of life into a positive contemporary description.

Suggested Responses:

Goddess	Lifestage	Positive aspect
Persephone	*Girl crossing the threshold of adolescence*	*She leaves home/achieves a new selfhood and goes off to college or gets married*
Demeter	*Mother experiencing "empty nest" syndrome*	*She sees new opportunities opening; returns to work and/or college*
Hecate	*Grandmother coming into her "golden years"*	*She shares the wisdom of life experiences with others who turn to her for guidance*

13. Follow-up creative writing activity: Ask students to use the Goddess Wheel information to develop a modern profile of the Goddess. This can be structured in essay form. Encourage students to brainstorm ideas and outline their profiles before putting them into paragraphs.

Each students' fictional character profile may be based on a single Greek goddess personality or on a combination of two or more goddesses. Instruct students to assign their characters contemporary fictional identities complete with names, professions, life styles, physical descriptions, pursuits, and interests that reflect their chosen Greek goddesses domains and concerns noted on the Wheel.

Have students read their finished modern profiles aloud and try to guess which original Greek goddesses were used as models. To discover if the class tends to use one particular goddess model over others, it may be fun to have someone tally which goddess prototype was used as they are read.

Name_____
Date_____

The Unity and Universality of the Goddess

Classify the six major Greek goddesses, Hera, Aphrodite, Persephone, Artemis, Demeter, and Athena, according to the characteristics inside the circle. Write the appropriate name(s) beside each characteristic.

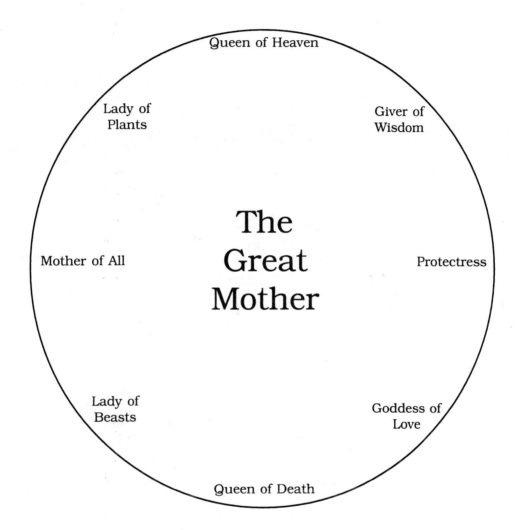

Name_____

Date_____

Dynamics of the Greek Goddesses

List the following information for each of the six major Greek goddesses:

The domain she presides over, the concerns involved in each domain that she is thought to be responsible for maintaining, and the symbolic representation she may take.

Goddess	Domain	Concerns	Symbolic Representations

Name_____
Date_____

The Goddess Wheel

Fill in the Goddess Wheel with the appropriate information about the six major Greek goddesses: name, domain, and concerns within that domain.

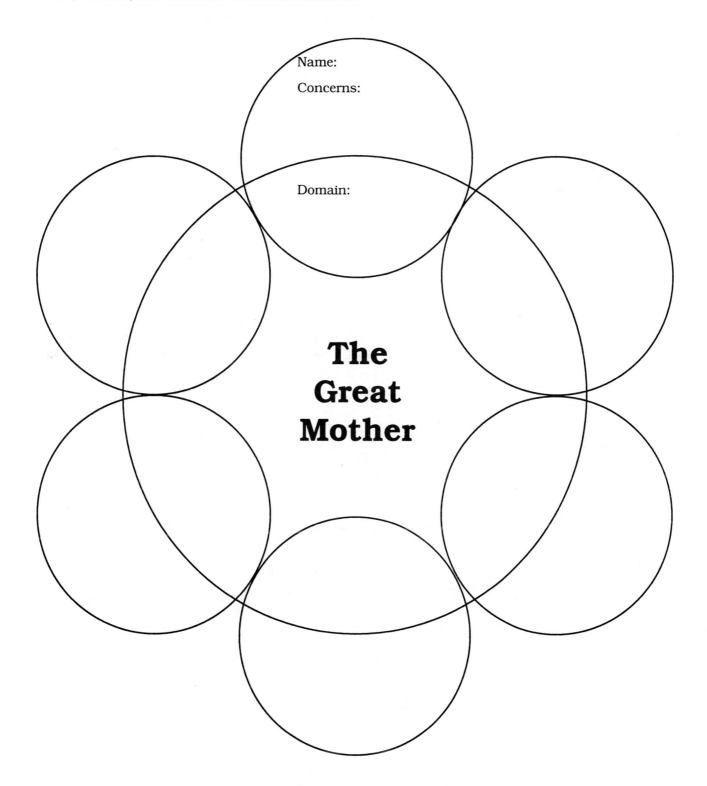

Lesson 5
Introduction to the Monomyth, an Initiation Theme

Objectives
- To become familiar with the archetypal hero figure's rite of passage known as the monomyth

- To generate examples of this monomyth as it appears in literature, myths, fairy tales, religious systems, and everyday life

Notes to the Teacher

Comparative mythologist Joseph Campbell put forward the idea of a threefold phase rite of passage called the "monomyth" which he observed operating in human cultures. (This concept was articulated earlier by Arnold van Gennep.) According to Campbell's analysis there is a dynamic archetypal pattern: (1) Separation, (2) Struggle/Initiation (3) Return/Reintegration that is played out in different contexts, such as sacred stories, myths, rituals, and dreams of individuals the world over. This experience is manifested in the archetypal figure of the hero or heroine involved in an adventure or vision quest. It is commonly referred to as an initiation scenario. Please refer to Campbell's classic study, *The Hero with a Thousand Faces*.[1] The chart on **Handout 12** may be a helpful visual aid to introduce students to this concept.

In the first phase of this archetype, the hero figure is separated from ordinary everyday surroundings and society and enters or descends into a different reality—a sacred space, supernatural realm, or alternate state of mind which can be viewed as a metaphorical "underworld"—where the candidate is forced to endure hardships, and sometimes tests. This journey into the underworld symbolizes the hero figure's exploration of his or her unconscious domain where one's terrors and deepest fears reside. The figure must triumph over these "demons" and overcome the ordeal in order to pass the initiation. Only then, may the initiate cross back over the threshold to emerge as a whole, regenerated person. The successful figure is then able to resume daily existence, but is reintegrated into society in a new way. The hero or heroine usually returns carrying a new

power or knowledge to bestow on society. This experience is in essence a dying to one's old existence and rising to new life (or more precisely, a new mode of life). Campbell likens this hero's or heroine's adventure to the coming of age trials that every young person must pass through on the way to becoming an adult. It is a pattern that can be seen operating universally in puberty ritual initiation ceremonies which are the subject of Lesson 6.

The best introduction to this concept is rendered by Joseph Campbell himself in his interview *The Power of Myth*—"The Hero's Adventure" episode. A class viewing of this video is urged to orient students to this material and to allow them to experience the visual expressions of these archetypes. By virtue of Campbell's masterful storytelling, this video is a very entertaining as well as educational approach to a complex and difficult subject. If the video is not available, read aloud to students from the text version.

The heroic figure has "a thousand faces" because Campbell encounters this monomyth sequence appearing again and again in a myriad of sacred stories and legends of various cultures and periods of human history. He goes so far as to note, "it might be said there is but one archetypal mythic hero whose life has been replicated in many lands by many, many people."[1] This prototype is often evident in the figure of "the founder," someone who institutes a new social order, religion, or way of life. Lesson 5 begins by asking students to look at an example of such a founder in the legend of Buddha. It goes on to feature other examples of the monomyth students have experienced in their previous readings of myth, folklore, and literature.

One classic reference to these themes being played out in fairy tales can be found in Bruno Bettelheim's *The Uses of Enchantment*. In his chapter, "The Struggle for Maturity," Bettelheim considers this psychological process as "the only way to master one's fate and win one's kingdom." He likens the folktale hero or heroine

---

[1] Joseph Campbell, *The Hero with a Thousand Faces*, (Princeton: Princeton University Press, 1977), 30.

to the successful initiate. He sees both these figures emerging from the "sacred voyage" having earned the ability to "truly become him/herself, the hero/heroine has become worthy of being loved." Bettelheim distinguishes between fairy tale and myth in the chapter, "Optimism versus Pessimism," which may provide some helpful insights at this point in the unit.[2]

Procedure

1. Introduce the Monomyth configuration to students as a threefold process involving a hero's or heroine's Separation, Struggle and Reintegration into society. (See Notes to the Teacher for background.) Distribute **Handout 12** to visually illustrate the Monomyth and chart the process with the class.

2. Distribute **Handout 13**. Read the story of young Siddhartha Gautama aloud with students. Distribute **Handout 14** and ask students to identify the three phases as they apply to this founder figure.

   Suggested Response:

   1. Separation: *Siddhartha leaves his kingdom to embark on his search for enlightenment. After dismissing the realms of hedonistic and aescetic pursuits as means to enlightenment, he retires to sit beneath the bodhi tree where he enters into an alternate state of mind.*

   2. Struggle-Initiation: *He encounters all manner of temptation and personal trials while in this sacred space. He triumphs over these travails and arrives at a state of enlightenment characterized by rapture and bliss.*

   3. Return: *He returns to the world with a new name/identity, The Buddha.*

   4. Gift: *He shares his knowledge of the Way to enlightenment with the rest of humanity. He founds Buddhism.*

   (Note: For further insight into the Buddha story refer to Campbell's *The Power of Myth*, "The Hero's Adventure," pages 159–162.)

3. Explain that this monomyth pattern surfaces in a variety of genres: literature, folktales, religious traditions, films, and real life! (The next lesson involves this pattern as it surfaces in ritual initiations.)

   Select a figure from one category that your students are familiar with from previous study to illustrate this process. Using the board or other visual aid, lead the class through the entire monomyth description for the chosen figure. Have students use **Handout 14** to record their answers under the correct heading. (See suggested responses on page 35.) Do not complete the last entry, "Resident college student," as it will be used as a transition to Lesson 6 to introduce the theme of initiation. See Notes to the Teacher for reference sources.) Some examples of classic heroic figures who exemplify this archetype include Moses, Herakles, Joan of Arc, and Hiawatha.

4. Small group or homework activity: Allow students to work on their own to complete **Handout 14** with figures of their own choosing for the categories given. Remind students that the gifts the figures return with are not always clearly deliniated in concrete objects; sometimes they bring back new potentials or capabilities. For example, the heroine in the fairytale "Beauty and the Beast" emerges from her ordeal with the capacity to love and be loved. Ask students to share answers in a large group discussion.

5. **Optional Activity:** Ask students to review films where heroes experience the monomyth process and have them independently deliniate each phase as well as the gift that the hero returns with to share with society. There are many popular films that develop this monomyth theme (i.e., *Little Buddha, Star Wars, Joy Luck Club, Room with a View*).

[2] Bruno Bettelheim, *The Uses of Enchantment: The Meaning and Importance of Fairytales*, (New York: Random House Vintage Books, 1977), 35–41.

Suggested Responses, Handout 14:

Hero Figure	Separation	Struggle/Initiation	Return/ Reintegration	Gift/New Power
Founder figure Prince Siddhartha Gautama	Leaves Kingdom—embarks on search; retires beneath bodhi tree where he enters an alternate state of mind	Encounters all manner of trials and temptation; triumphs over all and arrives at state of enlightenment characterized by rapture and bliss	Persuaded to return to the world, as Buddha, the enlightened	Shares his knowledge of the Way and founds Buddhism
Fairytale/ Folktale Hero/ Heroine Snow White	Spared from being killed; deserted in the forest; finds shelter with the dwarfs	Learns how to work well keeping house; succumbs to temptation by the evil queen in disguise; "dies" and is encased in a glass coffin where she rests for a long time (represents a period of inner growth)	Awakened by the prince, she disgorges the poison apple and comes to life (rebirth symbolizing an entry into a higher stage of development)	Reaches maturity; ready for marriage
Mythic Hero/ Heroine Odysseus	Lost at sea on the journey home from the war	Gets waylaid; encounters many forces both harmful and helpful while trying to return, including a sidetrip to Hades, the underworld, to consult Tiresias	After being shipwrecked, undergoes a rebirthing as he is washed up on the shores of Ithaca, his home country	Restores order to home; renews marriage and his parental role; embarks on new quest
Literary Hero/ Heroine Ebenezer Scrooge	Enters into a series of dreams/ alternate reality: Past, Present, Future on Christmas Eve	Visited by three spirits of Christmas who guide him through these visions pleasant and painful, and who seek to enlighten him	Awakens on Christmas morning transformed, filled with goodwill and intentions to make restitution for past wrongs committed	Exemplifies the true spirit of Christmas by sharing his wealth and giving of himself
Resident college student	Leaves home/ community to enter college	Experiences many trials (exams, personal/social decisions); if successful, he/she graduates	Following commencement, the young adult returns to society (either hometown or new community)	Shares his or her new knowledge and skills in concrete ways (employed, marriage, raising children) or gives back in less tangible ways (living ethically, serving as a role model)

Name_____
Date_____

Monomyth Process

Below is an illustration of the Monomyth. Chart the process with your teacher and the class.

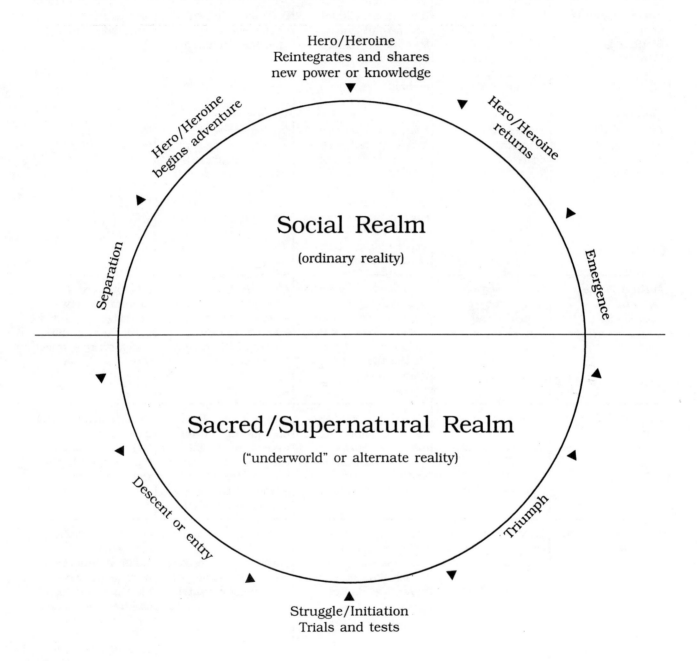

Monomyth in Legend:
The Story of the Buddha

Read through the following description of the Monomyth process as exemplified in the life of Prince Siddhartha Gautama who becomes The Buddha, or the founder of Buddhism. Then, try to identify the three phases of the process: Separation, Struggle/Initiation, Return/Re-integration, and the Gift. Note the phases on the chart, under the category "Founder," on **Handout 14**.

Siddhartha Gautama was a Hindu prince who lived from 563 to 483 BCE (before the common era) in India. According to legend, Siddhartha led a very sheltered life until one day, while riding outside the palace, he came across "Four Passing Sights" (these were age, suffering, death, and sacrifice in monkhood). Up until this moment, the prince had been carefully shielded from these brutal realities. He was determined to discover for himself the meaning of life, so foresaking his princely existence of pleasure and indulgence, he embarked on an existential quest for true enlightenment. After a long period of seeking out wisdom from master yogis and engaging in rigorous ascetic disciplines of self denial with other monks and almost expiring in the course of fasting, Siddhartha came to reject this approach. Having dismissed the realm of hedonistic pleasure in his princely life and the realm of austerity in his monkhood as a means to enlightenment, he vowed to sit beneath the bodhi tree and meditate until enlightenment came to him. The following passages are based on legendary accounts of what transpired during this cosmic transformation:

> The Evil One realizing that his antagonist's [Siddhartha's] success was imminent, rushed to the spot to disrupt his concentrations. He attacked first in the form of Kama, the God of desire, parading three voluptuous women with their tempting retinues. When the Buddha-to-be remained unmoved, the Tempter switched his guise to that of Mara, the Lord of death. His powerful hosts assailed the aspirant with hurricanes, torrential rains, and showers of flaming rocks, but Guatama had so emptied himself of his finite self that the weapons found no target to strike and turned into flower petals as they entered his field of concentration. When, in final desperation, Mara challenged his right to do what he was doing, Guatama touched the earth with his right fingertip, whereupon the earth responded, thundering "I bear you witness" with a hundred, a thousand, and a hundred thousand roars. Mara's army fled in rout, and the god's of heaven descended in rapture to tend the victor with garlands and perfumes. Thereafter, while the Bo Tree rained red blossoms that full-mooned night, Gautama's meditation deepened through watch after watch until, as the morning star glittered in the transparent sky of the east, his mind pierced at last the bubble of the universe and shattered it to naught, only, wonder of wonders, to find it miraculously restored with the effulgence of true being. The great Awakening had arrived. Gautama's being was transformed, and he emerged the Buddha. The event was of cosmic import. All created things filled the morning air with their rejoicings and the earth quaked six ways with wonder.[3]

> Then for seven days Gautama—now the Buddha, the enlightened—sat in motionless bliss; for seven days he stood apart and regarded the spot on which he had received enlightenment . . . and meditated on the doctrine of the sweetness of Nirvana . . . then he doubted whether his message could be communicated, and he thought to retain the wisdom for himself; but the god, Brahma descended from the zenith to implore that he should become the teacher of gods and men. The Buddha was thus persuaded to proclaim the path. And he went back into the cities of men where he moved among the citizens of the world bestowing the inestimable boon of the knowledge of the Way.[4]

[3] Huston Smith, *The World's Religions*, (New York: HarperCollins, 1991), 86.
[4] Joseph Campbell, *Hero with a Thousand Faces*, (Princeton, New Jersey: Princeton University Press, 1973), 33–34.

Name_____

Date_____

Monomyth—Examples

Identify the three phases of the Monomyth as they apply to Prince Siddhartha Guatama, The Buddha. Identify the three phases for a figure selected by your teacher. Then, fill in the mythic hero/heroine and the literary hero/heroine with figures of your own choice.

Hero Figure	Separation	Struggle/ Initiation	Return/ Reintegration	Gift/ New Power
Founder figure				
Fairytale Hero/ Heroine				
Mythic Hero/ Heroine				
Literary Hero/ Heroine				
Resident college student				

Lesson 6
Male and Female Initiation Rituals— The Monomyth in Action

Objectives
- To see how the three phase monomyth pattern operates within male and female initation rituals
- To make a presentation and/or write a reflection paper on modern initiation rituals

Notes to the Teacher
Now that the students have been introduced to the concept of the monomyth as it applies to archetypal heroes and heroines, they should be ready to apply this model to examples of actual initiation rituals as portrayed in different societies, including their own. Again, Joseph Campbell is an excellent source to refer to for this discussion. In his interview, *The Power of Myth*, "The Hero's Adventure," he likens the monomyth of the mythic hero or heroine to the "fundamental psychological transformation" each young person must undergo to become an adult. He says, "that's the basic motif of the universal hero's journey leaving one condition and finding the source of life to bring you forth into a richer or mature condition."[1]

Mircea Eliade, history of religions scholar, identifies three categories of intiation: (1) *puberty rites* in which the candidate is inducted into the adult cultural mode and is introduced to spiritual values; (2) *induction into a secret society* which usually requires uncommon comittment and mental or physical strength to pass through the ordeals; and (3) *discovering a mystical vocation* which demands a mastery of instruction and often takes on "ecstatic" dimensions by inducing trances and visionary experiences. Two texts by Eliade which provide a more detailed description of such rituals for the teacher are "Initiation and the Modern World" in *The Quest*, and *Rites and Symbols of Initiation: The Mysteries of Birth and Rebirth*.

Lesson handouts give a sample of different types of initiation ritual for students. The first example, from a primitive tribal tradition, looks at the process of male candidates being inducted into a new stage of life with a puberty rite. The second example looks at the monomyth process as experienced by female initiates into a society of shamanesses in Japan. The process of initiation described in these lessons is very similar to the "other worldly" experiences that shaman figures undergo for the benefit of their group. A good study of the concept of "shaman" is *The Shaman's Doorway* by Stephen Larsen.

While male initiation rituals have been documented extensively there are few studies which treat the female initiation adequately. One of the best studies of specifically female initiation rituals is Bruce Lincoln's *Emerging from the Chrysalis: Studies in Rituals of Women's Initiation*. Teachers may want to refer to this as a supplementary text. Lincoln's introduction and his concluding chapter are especially helpful. He writes that women's initiation is distinct from men's in that "rather than changing women's status, initation changes their fundamental being." Lincoln sees the pattern of female initation as "one of growth or magnification, an expansion of powers, capabilities, experiences."[2] Another interesting look at the forces beneath the female initiation archetype can be found in *Women Who Run With the Wolves* by Clarissa Pinkola Estes, Ph.D.

Procedure
1. Discuss the concept of initiation with students. Ask if any students have undergone initiation rituals in their own life experience. If so, will they share them? Discuss the potential distinction, if they see any, between male and female ritual initiations. Lead the discussion to consider the modern

---

[1] Joseph Campbell, "The Hero's Adventure," *The Power of Myth*, (New York: Doubleday, 1988), 124.
[2] Bruce Lincoln, *Emerging from the Chrysalis: Studies in Rituals of Women's Initiation*, (Cambridge: Harvard University Press, 1981), 103–104.

day pattern of leaving home and entering college as a possible initiation scenario. Have students fill in the last entry for **Handout 14**, resident college student. Suggested responses are included on the Teacher Answer key for **Handout 14**.

2. Explain to the students that the primary purpose for the young person's undergoing this experience is to become inducted into another stage of life. It symbolically represents the youth's life, death, and rebirth. Stress the importance of the new power or knowledge the initiate brings back from the ordeal to benefit or somehow serve his or her community.

3. Introduce students to Mircea Eliade's three types of initiation rituals. (See Notes to the Teacher.) Distribute **Handout 15**. Read through this example of an initiation ritual in a primal religion. Have students decide which of Eliade's types is represented in this passage.

Suggested Response:

Puberty rites as it involves the transition from boy status to man status within this culture.

4. Work with students to identify the three aspects of this monomyth. (A discussion can be found in Eliade's text, *Rites and Symbols*, pages 21–25.) Illustrate answers on the board.

Suggested Responses:

1. Separation—The young men are removed from their village homes and taken into the forest by the men of their tribe. Great bull-roarer noisemakers and histrionics by the women accompany this departure. The initiates are taken to a secret lodge deep in the forest. Pigs are sacrificed and eaten.

2. Struggle/Initiation—The young men undergo the circumcision operation and remain in the lodge for several months. They weave baskets and play sacred flutes to fill their isolation.

3. Return/Reintegration—The young men are removed from the lodge and taken to the sea to bathe. After having their bodies decorated, they return to the village keeping their eyes shut. Only when they are touched on the face with a "bull-roarer" may they complete their return with a feast.

5. Discuss with students what might be the new power or gift the men bring back from their ordeal, as it is not stated definitively in this account of the ritual.

Suggested Response:

They have emerged with a new status, manhood. Now, they are ready to take their place as men in the society. (This is a good point to emphasize to students that these phases are a general model for the rite of passage and each ritual or myth may not fit exactly into the formula.)

6. Distribute **Handout 16**. Discuss the meaning of shamaness with students. (See Notes to the Teacher on "shaman.") Have students read the account of the initiation ritual of the *mika* shamanesses of Japan. (Further insight into female initiation can be found in the Eliade text, *Rites and Symbols*, pages 41–51.) Have students write answers to the five questions.

Suggested Responses:

1. It fits into Eliade's categories of secret society initiation and mystical vocation initiation.

2. Earlier in her life, the candidate was separated from her family for training. At this initiation, she is marked as separate by wearing a white dress.

40

3. *White in this religion connotes death. White dress in our Western marriage connotes joy (purity).*

4. *Water is used to revive the shamaness from the blackout. Answers will vary on comparing the two initiation rituals.*

5. *Communication with the spirits of the dead, a highly prized ability in this religion*

7. **Evaluation Activity:** Quiz students on the monomyth process for the shamanesses.

   Suggested Responses:

   1. Separation—*Earlier in life, the candidate left her family and entered training. She is marked off in this ceremony by wearing white.*

   2. Struggle/Initiation—*The young candidate falls into a trancelike, alternate state of consciousness. She endures the possession experience and then is dashed with water a significant number of times.*

   3. Return/Reintegration—*The initiated shamaness is revived and thus "reborn" to her new vocation which is commemorated by changing into wedding apparel. She participates in a traditional wedding ceremony with her patron deity as groom. A celebration feast with her family and friends is held as she exhibits her new powers for them.*

8. **Optional Activities:** Have students choose one of the following topics to research and make a presentation and/or write a reflection paper:

   • Modern Symbols of Initiation

   a. Find a physical symbol used in conducting an initiation ritual in modern life.

   b. Research its origin and purpose as well as its function in the ritual.

   c. Present the object and background information in class as an oral report.

Note: This assignment *can* but does not necessarily have to feature a religious initiation such as a confirmation or a bar mitzvah. It could represent a secular initiation experience such as entering the military service or induction into a student society or club. (An excellent example of the latter can be seen in the popular film, *Dead Poets Society.*)

   • Modern Initiation Ceremony

   a. Observe firsthand a ritual initiation from a religious tradition or a secular group. Describe the ceremony and research the meaning of the symbols involved in the ritual.

   b. Read about a modern initiation ritual from outside of your own experience and write a reflection paper in which you consider the meaning of the symbols and behavior enacted.

Note: A "reflection" paper differs from a research paper in that it does not presuppose as much outside reading and research. This type of paper is meant to engage the student in a kind of personal discussion about the topic rather than require a dry rendition of factual information.

Male Initiation

Read through the following description of an initiation ritual from a primal religion:

> At the appointed time, the young candidates are taken by the men of the tribe into the forest. The bull-roarers—flat elliptical pieces of wood, which when twirled make an unearthly roaring sound—are booming. (Significantly, the word *balum* means both bull-roarer and ghost.) The women of the tribe look on from a distance, anxious and weeping, for they have been told the boys are to be eaten by a balum or ghostly monster, who will release them only on condition of receiving a sufficient number of pigs. The women have therefore been fattening pigs since the ceremony was announced, and hope they will be adequate to redeem their sons and lovers. There must be one pig for each initiate.
>
> Deep in the forest, the boys are taken to a secret lodge designed to represent the belly of the monster. A pair of eyes are painted on the entrance, and roots and branches betoken the horror's hair and backbone. As they approach he "growls"—the voice of more hidden bull-roarers.
>
> The pigs are sacrificed and eaten by the men and boys, for the monster demands only their "souls." The boys enter the lodge and undergo the circumcision operation. They remain in seclusion three or four months living in that long hut, inside the "monster." During this time they weave baskets and play two sacred flutes. These flutes are said to be male and female and to be married to each other. No women may see these flutes, and they are employed only during such sacred seasons as this.
>
> At the end of the seclusion period, the boys return to the village, but in a special manner which bespeaks festival and rebirth. They are first taken to bathe in the sea, and then are elaborately decorated with paint and mud. As they go back to the village, they must keep their eyes tightly shut. An old man touches each on the forehead and chin with a bull-roarer. They are then told to open their eyes, and then they may feast and talk to the women.[3]

[3] Robert Ellwood, *Many Peoples, Many Faiths: An Introduction to Religious Life of Mankind*, (New York: Prentice-Hall Inc., 1976), 36–37.

Name_____
Date_____

Female Initiation

Read the following account of the initiation ritual of the mika shamanesses of Japan, then answer the five questions below.

Blind girls became apprentices of older shamanesses at six or eight years of age. After a strict training involving fasts, cold-water ablutions, observing taboos, and learning shamaness songs and techniques of trance and divination, they were initiated.

For this rite, the novice wears a white robe called the death dress. She sits facing her mistress and other shamanesses; these elders sing and chant formulae and names of deities. Suddenly the mistress cries, "What diety possessed you?" When the candidate gives the name of a god or Buddha or bodhisattva (who will thereafter be her main supernatural patron), the mistress throws a rice cake at her, causing her to fall onto the floor in a faint.

The elders then dash water onto her head as many as 3,333 times. Then they lie beside her and revive her with body heat. When she finally comes to, she is said to be reborn; she exchanges the death dress for wedding apparel, and a traditional Japanese wedding—with traditional exchange of cups of sake (rice wine) nine times—is performed. The new shamaness is the bride, her diety the groom.

Next a great feast of celebration follows, shared by relatives and friends of the new medium; she demonstrates her proficiency at communicating with spirits of the dead. (For a week following, as a sort of divine honeymoon, she may live alone in a shrine with her diety).[4]

1. This ritual of the mika shamanesses falls into which two of Eliade's three categories of intiation rituals?

2. Identify the separation aspect of this ritual.

3. What is the significance of the white dress in this religion? Compare the significance of a white dress in an American wedding.

4. What is the importance of water in this ritual? How does the ordeal in this initiation differ from that in the male puberty rite studied in **Handout 15**?

5. Identify the new found power or benefit the shamaness bride brings with her.

[4] Ibid, 50.

Lesson 7
An Alternate Initiation Theme—
Liberation of Transcendence

Objectives

- To become acquainted with examples of fictional characters undergoing the liberation of trancendence experience

- To uncover several similarities and differences between the characters' experiences

Notes to the Teacher

This lesson turns the attention from rituals of initation to literary analysis of an alternate initiation theme: liberation of transcendence. It instructs students to look at this theme as it is depicted in two extended prose passages from twentieth-century literature: the chapter entitled "Sophistication" from Sherwood Anderson's *Winesberg, Ohio* and the end of section four of James Joyce's *Portrait of the Artist as a Young Man* beginning, "He could wait no longer," and ending " . . . and the tide was flowing in fast to the land with a low whisper of her waves, islanding a few last figures in distant pools." (pages 164–173 of the Penguin Book paperback edition, 1977) The teacher will have to secure the Anderson and Joyce passages for the activities in this lesson.

Students will delve into the archetypal aspects of these fictional accounts of youth standing on the threshold of adulthood. It is certainly a stage of life that your students will identify with despite the difference in context. The theme encountered in this lesson is well-articulated by Joseph Henderson in his contributing chapter, "Ancient Myths and Modern Man," to the Jungian text *Man and His Symbols*. Henderson identifies a secondary type of initiation scenario working in the human psyche as "the liberation of transcendence." Further references to his insightful study of initiation scenarios can be found in *The Wisdom of the Serpent: The Myths of Death, Rebirth and Resurrection* co-authored by Henderson and Maud Oakes. This type of initiation scenario differs profoundly in style and content from the Monomyth process exemplified in the hero's or heroine's adventure/puberty rituals of initiation that were the topic of lessons 5 and 6. While both the monomyth and the liberation initiation scenarios involve a leavetaking which serves to usher the immature individual into adulthood, they do so by different means and to different ends.

The initiatory events previously studied as the Monomyth involve a rite of passage whereby the individual dies to his or her earlier existence and is reborn into a new identity. Through the monomyth process, the successful candidate is temporarily separated and undergoes a tremendous ordeal to emerge more integrally bonded to his or her original community, although assuming a new role. By contrast, the liberation theme, which is the subject of this lesson, is a transcendent experience whereby the adolescent individual takes flight from the old order and emerges a more psychologically integrated adult ready and able to blaze his or her own life path. Where the monomyth ritual serves to reconnect the person to his or her community in a new way, the initiation scenario known as liberation of transcendence serves to *separate* the newly integrated person from the family and/or hometown (either literally by physically moving away, as George does at the end of *Winesburg Ohio*, or psychologically by rejecting the family expectation to become a priest, as Stephen does in *Portrait of the Artist as a Young Man*.) Once this liberation of transcendence flight is successfully navigated, the young adult directs him or herself out into the world to meet the destiny that he or she creates. Henderson speaks of this type of initiation:

> It is a journey of release, renunciation and atonement, presided over and fostered by some spirit of compassion . . . Not only the flight of birds or journey into the wilderness represent this symbolism, but any strong movement exemplifying release. In the first part of life, when one is still attached to the original family and social group, this may be experienced as that moment of initiation at which one must learn to take the decisive steps into life alone.[1]

---

[1] Joseph Henderson, "Ancient Myths and Modern Man," *Man and His Symbols*, Carl Jung, ed., (New York: Doubleday, Aldus Books, 1964), 152.

Thus, through this type of initiation the children are set free from the limiting framework they were born into and are ready (as the old fairy tales say) "to seek their fortune." The life story the young people now compose will be based on the choices they make and on what internal resources they can muster, rather than on what they were assigned at birth.

Procedure

1. Engage students in a discussion centering on the theme of liberation. Point out the distinction between seeking freedom actively and running away from something. If necessary, introduce the concept of transcendence using concrete symbolic examples, such as explorers venturing into unknown regions (Antarctic or space). Other symbolic figures that represent this state are winged creatures: birds, mythological dragons, and other trancendent realities, such as the spiritual pilgrimages of Henry David Thoreau, and manifestations of the Greek god Hermes.

2. Ask students to read "Sophistication" silently or orally. Distribute **Handout 17** and form students into small groups to answer the five questions and discuss this passage in terms of the liberation of transcendence theme. (See Notes to the Teacher.)

   Suggested Responses:

   1. *(pages 234–235) The passage beginning, "There is a time in the life of every boy when he for the first time takes the backward view of life . . . " through, "He wants, most of all, understanding.": At such a moment, memories come into play as the "limitations of life" become apparent. A person becomes reflective and begins to question himself or herself—senses the futility of life and begins to feel his or her own mortality. At such a moment an individual may seek solace in the company of another human being.*

   2. *George is in between boyhood and manhood, likewise Helen is not a girl but not yet fully a woman. Maturity involves realizing in Anderson's own words ones "own insignificance in the scheme of existence" and continuing to affirm life in spite of it. This affirmation may take the form of a love relationship and/or a pursuit of a professional ambition. Yes, both characters are growing into adulthood; they harbor the same need, to love and be loved. They are beginning to affirm their own life and seek out their own life direction.*

   4. *The setting of the chapter is a perfect backdrop for the mood of the story at this point. It opens as night is falling: the time is the late autumn of the year; the place is a small town in the American Heartland. The night is warm and pleasant. The air is dusty with decaying leaves. Thus, the time is ripe for a transformation. It is the end of the year, the light is fading, and the landscape is dusty, all of which mirror George's frame of mind. He's feeling "old and tired." Three symbols or metaphors:*

   (a) page 234: George is described "like a leaf blown by the wind," which illustrates the transitory nature of life.

   (b) page 237: George is remembering a previous walk with Helen in early summer, their "talk beside the field of young corn," and the sense of shame due to his young boasting. The unripe corn symbolizes their immature stage of life.

   (c) pages 239–241: The deserted fairground scene with its "ghosts" of people who passed through earlier in the day is now silent and dark. The author says being in such a place brings out the reflective side of one's nature. It indicates both the absurdity ("meaninglessness of life") and the sublime beauty ("one loves life so intensely") of life.

   Note the following contrast in the final paragraph: The author juxtaposes the images of George and Helen playing "like two splendid young things in a young world" against the setting of night, during the darkest time of the year, amid dusty fields of dry corn. In other words, vitality and youthful promise are set against death and a decaying landscape.

   5. *(See Notes to the Teacher for a full description.) Liberation of transcendence: initiation process involving a personal flight experience whereby a young person frees himself or herself from the constraints put upon him or her by childhood*

46

family/home and seeks out his or her own way or life goals. This chart may be helpful to illustrate the differences between the two initiation scenarios.

Monomyth vs.	Liberation of Transcendence
Means: *Ritual process of Separation– Struggle– Return/Reintegration*	Means: *Personal flight experience with moment of truth or revelation ("epiphany")*
End: *Emerge with gift for society and/ or new role to fulfill in original community*	End: *Emerge with a new, more fully integrated self and ready to pursue a self-chosen life direction or goal*

3. Possible comparative activity: Have students read the end of section four from *Portrait of the Artist As a Young Man* and uncover the flight symbols and liberation theme in this context. Working in their small groups, ask students to complete the following:

   (1) review the "Sophistication" passage from *Winesburg, Ohio* along with the given passage from *Portrait of the Artist as a Young Man*

   (2) identify *five similarities* and *five differences* in these two fictional accounts of a "liberation of transcendence" initiation scenario

   Students may require some prompting initially.

   Suggested Responses:
   Similarities

   1. *George and Stephen are both on the verge of a new adventure or are entering a new life stage.*

   2. *Both remove themselves physically on the eve of their liberation to contemplate the change.*

   3. *Both experience female figures as representing compassion and inspiration.*

   4. *Both experience insight into the meaning of their lives and futures.*

   5. *Mother Goddess symbols are featured in both passages in the images of "climbing of a hill" at nightfall.*

   Differences

   1. *George is going away to work as a journalist in the city; Stephen is going to attend the university rather than become a priest.*

   2. *George starts off alone and meets up with his friend Helen; Stephen takes his flight alone and encounters friends along the way and later a beautiful female figure.*

   3. *Stephen's journey employs literal flight symbols and the metaphor of a flower opening, whereas George's metaphor is a leaf blown in the wind.*

   4. *Stephen hears the call of life to his soul, instead of the call to priesthood duty; George hears the message of the limitations of life and death and seeks out a female friend to comfort him.*

   5. *The Mother Goddess symbol of the crescent moon appears in Stephen's final scene; Mother Goddess images of "the enlightenment beneath the tree" and her agricultural symbol, dry corn fields, pervade George's night journey.*

   Ask each group to share their analysis with the rest of the class.

4. In a concluding full-class discussion ask students to consider which passage is more optimistic, in their opinion. Have students think about why these flight experiences were necessary in order for the characters to move on to a different life phase. Ask students to surmise if these characters will be successful in their new enterprises. (At this point, you may wish to direct students to complete the final chapter of *Winesburg, Ohio*, "Departure," and/or to read further in *Portrait of the Artist As a Young Man* to see how the author resolves these characters' transformations.)

"Sophistication"

Read through the chapter "Sophistication" in *Winesburg, Ohio* by Sherwood Anderson, and answer the following questions.

1. Describe the "moment of sophistication" that comes to George, using the words of the author. Then, put this experience into your own words and life context.

2. Analyze the final statements of this short story: "For some reason they could not have explained they had both got from their silent evening together the thing needed. Man or boy, woman or girl, they had for a moment taken hold of the thing that makes the mature life of men and women in the modern world possible."

   In your opinion, is George a boy or a man? Is Helen a girl or a woman? Why? What traits constitute a person becoming an adult? Do either of these characters possess these traits? Be specific.

3. Describe the transformation these characters are undergoing in terms of your own life experience. Can you identify with any of their thoughts, feelings, or impressions? Explain.

4. How does the setting contribute to the mood of the story? Select three symbols that stand out in the passage and explain how the author uses them.

5. Arrive at a description of the archetype liberation of transcendence. How does this theme compare with the earlier initiation scenario you studied as the monomyth?

Lesson 8
The Archetypal Image of Flight—
A Personal Account

Objective
- To write an autobiographical account of a personal flight experience

Notes to the Teacher
This lesson uses the archetypal theme of liberation introduced in Lesson 7 as a basis for an autobiographical student narrative. While this includes a structured writing format, the teacher can decide the usefulness of the steps, given students' abilities. The writing process should be adapted and geared to the level of the students. While this writing process might seem formulaic and lengthy, it integrates reading, writing, and language skills. Through these steps the students are given a chance to generate and clarify their ideas, review each other's work, and have a clearer picture of "what the teacher is looking for" in this assignment.

Joseph Henderson's chapter, "Ancient Myths and Modern Man," in *Man and His Symbols*, ends with a passage speculating on the meaning of these flight images in our lives. It would be helpful to share these profound insights directly with the class by reading the passage to them.

The archetypal pattern known as initiation has formed the core of this unit on archetypes. This material has special relevance to the students in the age group of the advanced placement and honors levels. The initiation process outlined in these lessons should mesh with experiences students are undergoing at this time in their lives. This may be a good place to point out to them that these motifs do not pertain exclusively to their current stage of life. Rather, these symbols and themes known as archetypes have a way of surfacing again and again in different forms throughout our lives. If recognized when encountered again, they can serve as helpful guideposts to mark the way through other difficult passages.

This lesson is an attempt to help the students synthesize their new understanding of the liberation of transcendence initiation theme as expressed in the archetype of flight. They are asked to integrate this theme into a writing activity which draws from personal experience.

Procedure
1. Tell students that you want them to reflect on their own life experiences of the concepts discussed in Lesson 7. Explain that you want them to write an autobiographical account of a flight experience. For the purposes of this lesson, they can write about either a transcendent experience or a flight of escape. This experience can be a physical and/or spiritual journey that they have actually taken or have taken in their imagination.

2. As an example of a type of personal flight journey taken in a person's imagination, distribute **Handout 18**, the Edna St. Vincent Millay poem "Departure." After reading the poem with students, lead a discussion about the impulse behind the poet's desire to break away as a rebellion against the conventions of her daily life. Note that this is a somewhat different impulse from the *transcendent* initiation flight journeys undertaken by George and Helen and Stephen in the passages previously studied. The experience of the speaker in the "Departure" poem is not an initiation. Through it, she does not deliver herself from her circumstances or somehow change her lot in life. Rather, she uses her wonderful imagination to take a temporary sojourn from her everyday world and then returns to her original role of the dutiful daughter at the end. You may wish to discuss with students some possible reasons why the young speaker in this poem does not act on the flight impulse at this time (immaturity, fear, uncertainty, sense of obligation). An example of Millay's own rapturous flight journey of transcendence is conveyed in her signature poem, "Renascence," complete with the archetypal death and rebirth theme. You may wish to have students look into this reference.

3. Distribute **Handout 19**, the narrative writing assignment and prewriting sheet. Read over the assignment with students and allow time for brainstorming in the prewriting sections.

4. Distribute the writing activity specification/evaluation sheet, **Handout 20**. Complete the handout with the students as a class. Have students supply the specifications for this sheet garnered from their assignment handout. Also designate points for each item so students will know their weight and indicate total points possible and how they will be translated into a grade.

Suggested Responses:

Type of writing—*narrative first person account of a flight experience*

Content to include:

1. *First person point of view*
2. *Setting—description*
3. *Motivation behind the experience*
4. *Metaphors of release*
5. *Conflict being grappled with internally and/or externally*

Mechanics to check for:

1. *Essay form—sequential and clear*
2. *(Language skill) To be taught after reviewing first draft*
3. *Grammar and punctuation*
4. *Spelling*
5. *Neatness*

5. Have students write first drafts and perform self checks according to the specification sheet.

6. Ask students to work in pairs to perform peer reviews according to the following steps:

Peer review steps

1. Students exchange papers and initial the top of the peer column with their own initials.

2. Read the paper and perform the following P.Q.P. response

   P = Praise: First, find something good to say about the paper.

   Q = Question: Ask questions about things you don't understand or that need to be clarified.

   P = Polish: Give suggestions as to how the writer might improve their narrative.

   (**Note:** Students may need to be reminded that these are suggestions and they are not obligated to integrate them all into their papers.)

3. Students should then go over the paper and check for each specification item and check or dash the space beside each item in the Peer column.

   (**Note:** Peers are not to grade the papers or issue points.)

7. Students return the narratives to their owners. Students are directed to revise their narratives to submit a first draft to the teacher. (This is not the final draft for grading.)

8. Collect and read over the students' drafts and look for common errors in mechanics to form the basis of a Language Skill Lesson (specification 2, under Mechanics). After teaching or reviewing this Language Skill, hand back the papers. Inform students that they are responsible for correcting their papers accordingly.

9. Collect the final draft along with the specification sheet. Give points according to specifications and translate these into a grade. Provide comments for students in the appropriate space.

Departure

It's little I care what path I take,
And where it leads it's little I care;
But out of this house, lest my heart break,
I must go, and off somewhere.

It's little I know what's in my heart,
What's in my mind it's little I know,
But there's that in me must up and start,
And it's little I care where my feet go.

I wish I could walk for a day and a night,
And find me at dawn in a desolate place
With never the rut of a road in sight,
Nor the roof of a house, nor the eyes of a face.

I wish I could walk till my blood should spout,
And drop me, never to stir again,
On a shore that is wide, for the tide is out,
And the weedy rocks are bare to the rain.

But dump or dock, where the path I take
Brings up, it's little enough I care;
And it's little I mind the fuss they'll make,
Huddled dead in a ditch somewhere.

"Is something the matter, dear," she said,
"That you sit at your work so silently?"
"No, mother, no, 'twas a knot in my thread.
There goes the kettle, I'll make tea."

—Edna St. Vincent Millay

Narrative Writing Assignment—
Personal Flight Experience

Write a first-person narrative account of a liberating flight that you personally have experienced or wish to experience at this point in your life. This can be an account of a physical and/or spiritual journey that you have undertaken in reality or have wanted to take in your imagination.

Before you write, you should think about what motivated you to take the flight. For example, were you running away from something or seeking something? Did fear or desire for adventure create the impulse? Describe where you went, how you got there, and what you encountered on your flight (description of places, people, and symbolic forms that appeared on your journey). Be sure to include metaphors and symbolic flight images to illustrate your experience. Identify the internal and/or external conflict you were struggling to resolve at this time and any insights you gained through the experience. Think about how you resolved your conflict; or, if it remained unresolved, how did the flight experience find closure?

Now write the story of your personal flight.

Prewriting:

Motivation for the flight	Setting/Other characters

Metaphors	Symbolic images

Conflicts in question internal/external	Resolution or closure to the flight

Name_____

Date_____

Specification—Evaluation Sheet

Type of writing _____

Students should include:	Self	Peer	Teacher
Content:			
1. _____			
2. _____			
3. _____			
4. _____			
5. _____			
Mechanics:			
1. _____			
2. _____			
3. _____			
4. _____			
5. _____			

Comments:

Lesson 9
The Benevolent Guide

Objectives

- To recognize the archetype of the benevolent guide

- To identify the function and role of the archetypal guide in a short-story

Notes to the Teacher

Having completed the introduction to the archetype of the hero or heroine initiate in its various manifestations, the last four lessons are devoted to an analysis of additional archetypal figures. In each lesson, students are asked to uncover the function and role of these figures as they appear in literature and myth. A first-rate supplementary resource for these last four chapters, as well as for the unit as a whole, can be found in the previously cited David Adams Leeming's Anthology, *The World of Myth.*

The first of these figures, the benevolent guide, is known by many different titles and takes many different guises. It is usually an older person, either male or female, who intervenes in a positive way to assist the hero or heroine in his or her quest or initiation journey. This archetype is familiar as the fairy godmother or wise old man in the fairy tales and folk legends of the world. This guardian spirit, or benevolent guide, serves to balance out the malevolent forces facing the hero or heroine and provide him or her with wise counsel and/or physical assistance to overcome ordeals. Merlin in the Arthurian Legends exemplifies this archetype, while a more contemporary version can be seen in the Obi-wan Kenobe character in the original *Star Wars* film. Carl Jung himself refers to the benevolent guide as the symbol of "supreme insight."

William Faulkner's short story, "The Bear," which is used to illustrate the benevolent guide figure in this lesson, is yet another example of an initiation scenario. It may be used as a directed reading activity as well as a review of the initiation themes seen in a different context. With this story, Faulkner, a master storyteller, allows us to view the development of a young man living in the American South as he embarks on a series of hunting trips over several years, between the ages of ten and fourteen. As Faulkner wrote several versions of this story—one which was later incorporated into a novella with the same title—it is imperative that the version which begins "He was ten," printed in the *Uncollected Stories of William Faulkner* edited by Joseph Blotner, be used with this lesson.

Procedure

1. Ask students to recount an incident from their own experience with hunting and primitive camping and/or an encounter with a wild animal. Discuss the allure big game hunting has held for people through the ages, beyond the purpose of obtaining food. If possible, show a visual of a bear and/or a video excerpt showing the magnificence and ferocity of this archetypal animal. Inform the class that this Faulkner short story, "The Bear," follows the development of a young man over the course of several years and features several archetypes, including one which will be the focus of this lesson. See if the class can surmise as they read the story which new archetype is under consideration.

2. Together, read the first section of "The Bear," up to the break on page 286. Ask students to take special note of the relationship between the boy protagonist and the character Sam Fathers. Discuss the details of the story on a literal level and allow students to become familiar with the Southern dialect peculiar to Faulkner's characters.

Section 1.

Discussion Questions: Ask the following questions to prompt discussion of setting, characters, archetypal symbols, and plot or use the questions as an assignment for comprehension review:

1. What new situation does the young protagonist find himself in as the story opens?

2. What dimensions does the bear character take on in the young boy's imagination? Can you think of any entities in your own life that take on such stature?

3. What are some indications that the bear is an archetype?

4. What role does Sam Fathers play in the boy's life?

5. What lessons does Sam Fathers teach the young boy in the initial section of the story?

Suggested Responses:

1. *The boy, having just turned ten, was allowed to accompany the other men folk on a hunting trip.*

2. *The bear takes on legendary dimensions, almost in the manner of a tall tale, by devouring dogs and calves and overcoming rifle shots at point blank range. This is definitely no ordinary bear; it has earned itself a proper name, Old Ben.*

3. *The bear haunts the boy's dreams. It takes on a towering mythic quality; it is a manifestation of "wilderness" itself and thus strikes fear in his heart. Moreover, it is primordial and shadowy—"an apotheosis" (Greek: apo=from + theos=god)—a figure raised to the status of a god. He likens the bear to the legendary Priam, the tragic last King of Troy. There's an indication that the bear is immortal.*

4. *Sam Fathers is like a surrogate father, as his name suggests. He serves as a teacher and hunting coach to the boy. First and foremost, while the young boy is learning the rudimentaries of shooting, Sam stands by him to see that he acts right and no harm befalls him at this immature stage.*

5. *Sam Fathers instructs the boy in shooting and hunting techniques and initiates him into the experience of the wilderness and the reality of the bear. They enter the forest following no trail and find themselves in a place the boy has never been before. (Have students note that this is the classic archetypal situation of the hero's initiation: leaving behind the familiar reality for the unknown and encountering a primordial force there. In this case, the young boy is not yet ready to make the trip on his own.)*

3. Follow-up activity and/or journal entry: Ask students to think over their own life experiences and have each of them write about a figure in his or her own life that served as a surrogate parent, or teacher/coach in the way that Sam Fathers does for the boy.

4. Ask students to identify the different archetypal figures as they read.

Suggested Responses:

Story Character	Archetype
Boy	*Hero to be initiated**
Sam Fathers	*Benevolent Guide*
Old Ben	*Primordial Beast, Fear, Wilderness*

*Suggest that students look for a monomyth configuration in this story, while at the same time reminding them that individual cases do not always fit neatly into the monomyth formula. Also encourage students to look for a transcendent flight experience which may surface in this story.

5. Distribute **Handout 21**. Ask students to complete the reading of the second section independently, up to the break on page 290 (this is the excerpt concerning the boy in his eleventh year), and complete the first two parts of the handout. Students may enjoy working on this handout in partners or small groups.

Suggested Responses:

1. Boy at age 10

   First hunting trip with men; first direct encounter with the bear

   Pre-adolescent male is inducted into the mysteries of the wilderness by a benevolent guide figure and discovers the reality of the bear, which previously existed larger-than-life in his childish vision.

   Boy taking his first excursions into manhood with the help of the benevolent guide.

2. Boy at age 11

Hunting trip the next year; boy out hunting with his own gun practicing his tracking skills.

Boy embarks alone on a trek into the woods to see the bear for the first time; he relinquishes all his aids, including his gun.

Boy making his first excursion into manhood alone.

3. Boy at age 14

Several years later; boy on annual hunting trip has new insight into the problem of meeting up with the bear. He returns alone the next spring to ambush the bear with the fyce dog.

Young man has acquired the skills and experience of a hunter. Having passed all the prerequisites and armed with the dog possessing the necessary spirit, the young man takes the bear by surprise, yet he allows the moment to pass without shooting.

Young man makes successful transition into manhood, confronts his primal fear without being destroyed or destroying it.

4. Final Scene

Father's office

Discussion between young man and his father concerning the final encounter with the bear, especially the questions as to why the son did not shoot.

Boy takes a place in man's world. He learns to value abstract virtues and embrace them as immutable truth.

He has learned by possessing courage, in addition to humility and pride; he has become worthy of his status as a man.

Answers will vary.

6. Discuss and/or quiz students on their literal understanding of Section 2.

Section 2.

Discussion Questions: Ask students to think about the advice Sam gives the boy.

1. Why is it necessary for the boy to leave the gun behind? What objects does he take with him on this foray into the woods? Why does he relinquish even these objects?

2. What three lessons does the boy remember to follow from Sam Father's teaching at this point in the story? Are they useful directions? Why?

3. What happens at this point in the story?

Suggested Responses:

1. *The compass, watch, and stick represent lifeless mechanical devices—grandfather's time piece and a stick to fend off snakes—which would not allow the boy to encounter the wilderness unaided.*

2. *The boy walked in one direction trying to complete a circle, then he walked in another circle in the opposite direction to bisect his footprints. Finally, he sat down in one place.*

3. *The wilderness coalesced and solidified; it came together in the figure of the bear. The boy sees the bear and confronts this creature without the gun or other talismans. He accomplishes his self-imposed test.*

7. Ask students to read sections 3 and 4 of "The Bear" and complete **Handout 21**. Read the first paragraph of section 3 aloud to note the following expression, "He had killed his buck, and Sam Fathers had marked his face with the hot blood . . ." This is an example of a direct ritual act performed by the guide to indicate the young boy has passed his hunting ordeal. Also note in this paragraph the significance of the young man surpassing his teacher by the statement, "He knew game trails that even Sam Father's did not know . . ." When this happens, the teacher has performed a noble service. On some levels the guide's work is completed and the child is ready to make his or her own way in the world. In this case, the boy must make his way in the "wilderness" to confront the primal nightmare figure of the bear.

8. Point out or ask students to find the key sentence of the story that encapsulates the boy's initiation rite-of-passage in a nutshell (found on page 290): "If Sam Fathers had been his mentor and the back-yard rabbits and squirrels at home his kindergarten, then the wilderness the old bear ran was his college, the old male bear itself, so long unwifed and childless as to have become its own ungendered progenitor, was his alma mater." Discuss the meaning of the word mentor and the importance of such a figure in a person's life, not just at adolescence but at every lifestage.

9. Discuss and/or quiz students on their literal understanding of section 3.

Section 3.

Discussion Questions:

1. Having confronted the bear alone, what is the boy's next self-imposed task? How do you know he is ready?

2. After his glimpse of the bear rushing past, what does the young man suddenly realize?

3. Why does this final encounter with the bear become "an ambush" rather than a "stalk"? Describe the literal action at this point of the story.

4. What is the significance of Sam's appearance at the end of this final encounter?

Suggested Responses:

1. *The boy is now fourteen years old and has acquired a remarkable amount of expertise in tracking and woodsmanship. He has passed the initiation of shooting a buck as well as an ordinary bear and has even applied his mentor's tribal techniques in hunting. He is ready for college, represented by the archetypal bear.*

2. *His epiphany* is that he has not brought along the right dog to help engage the bear.*

3. *The young man has all necessities and takes the bear by surprise. The fyce dog went for the bear, the bear rose on its hind legs, and yet the dog would not stop. The young man ran to save the dog, thowing away the gun in the process, and found himself under the looming bear figure like in his dreams. The bear departed.*

4. *Sam approaches with the boy's gun and remarks that the boy did not shoot even though he had the opportunity and ability. Remind the readers that there was a lot more at stake here than a trophy, setting the stage for the later discussion with his father.*

10. As a concluding activity, ask students to break into small groups to compose their own discussion questions for section 4 and exchange them with other small groups to answer.

11. In the wrap-up discussion, you may want to stress the personal values the young man works out for himself at the end of the story with his father's prompting and most importantly with the examples of Sam, the dog, and the bear to guide him.

12. Possible follow-up activity: Ask students to write a character sketch of Sam Fathers using the information in the story as a starting point and expanding on it if necessary.

*Students should be made aware of the literary term epiphany as a revelation or insight of sublime proportions usually attributed to James Joyce's characters.

"The Bear"

The short-story, "The Bear," can be divided into four sections corresponding to the changing ages of the young male protagonist and the stages along his unique initiation journey. Read each section, as instructed by your teacher, and fill in the information below.

Section 1.   pages 281–286   Boy at age 10

Setting:

Plot Summary:

Lifestage:

Section 2.   pages 296–290   Boy at age 11

Setting:

Plot Summary:

Lifestage:

Section 3.   pages 290–292   Boy at age 14

Setting:

Plot Summary:

Lifestage:

Section 4.   pages 292–293   Final Scene

Setting:

Plot Summary:

Father's assessment:

Son's assessment:

Student's assessment of the boy's accomplishments:

Lesson 10
The Sacred Marriage

Objectives
- To introduce students to the archetype of the sacred marriage
- To analyze the sacred marriage archetype in the context of a short story

Notes to the Teacher

This lesson uncovers another archetypal motif, the sacred marriage, in which two figures, a man and a woman, join together in a spiritual union of opposites to rejuvenate the cosmos. This motif is an ancient one and runs deep throughout the world's sacred stories and myths as well as literature. Joseph Henderson's chapter "Ancient Myths and Modern Man" in *Man and His Symbols* cites this archetype as "the heart of the initiation since its origins in the mystery-religions of antiquity." He uses the "Beauty and the Beast" tale to illustrate this as an especially significant female experience characterized by "a process of awakening."[1] Elinor Gadon discusses the origin and history of this archetype in chapter 8, "Sumer: The Descent of Inanna" in her comprehensive study *The Once and Future Goddess*. Though her analysis focuses on the archetype in the context of this particular Sumerian myth, certain generalizations can be made about roles played by the united couple.

The ritual enactment of the marriage ceremony is sacred. The female character assumes the part of the Earth Goddess and the male takes on the role of the vegetation god-king, synonymous with fruitfulness of the land (Sometimes this figure has attributes of the sky-god as well). The archetypal theme behind this god-king partner to the Goddess has an ancient model in agricultural cycle in which the god-king must die (be sacrificed) and be replanted to renew the fertility of the land and its people. This motif has been documented in Sir James Frazer's classic *The Golden Bough*. It is important to note here that in the reality of the participants and spectators of this sacred marriage, the two persons do not merely *play* the role of these deities, they literally become them for the duration of the ritual enactment. Thus, the power of the ceremony for believers should not be underestimated.

For the purposes of this lesson, the essence of this complex ritual is illustrated in the nineteenth century Nathaniel Hawthorne short story, "The Maypole of Merry Mount." As students may not be familiar with the maypole tradition or the historical context of this story, give them background in these areas if time allows. Scholar Mircea Eliade includes an illuminating analysis of the symbolism of "the may tree" in "Vegetation: Rites and Symbols of Regeneration" in *Patterns in Comparative Religion*. He refers to the principle behind this springtime sacred marriage of the May King and Queen as "the desire to spur on the circuit of biocosmic energy, and particularly vegetative energy, on a vast scale."[2] He goes on to identify the basis of this union as the sacred life force expressing itself in the cycle of growth, depletion, and regular regeneration. What Eliade sees happening in this archetype is a symbolic celebration of a cosmic occurance wherein the joining of the May King and Queen in marriage parallels the rejuvenation of the earth in spring.

Procedure

1. Introduce students to the background of the maypole traditions. (See Notes to the Teacher.) Suggest the current traditions of decorating Christmas trees and Easter trees—hanging plastic colored eggs on budding trees in early spring—as contemporary counterparts to the maypole celebrations. Discuss any other springtime nature celebrations (Earth day festivities) that commemorate the renewal of earth during this season.

2. Read the first paragraph of "The Maypole of Merry Mount" with the students. Ask them to identify the single sentence that foreshadows the conflict and summarizes the theme of this story. (*"Jollity and gloom were contending for an empire."*)

---

[1] Joseph Henderson, "Ancient Myths and Modern Man," *Man and His Symbols,* Carl Jung, ed. (New York: Doubleday, Aldus Books, 1964), 134; 137–140.
[2] Mircea Eliade, "Vegetation: Rites and Symbols of Regeneration," *Patterns in Comparative Religion* (Kansas City: Sheed and Ward Inc., 1958), 309–315.

3. Ask students to read the rest of the Hawthorne short story. Distribute **Handout 22**. Lead a discussion of any archetypes that may have surfaced in their reading and record them, or have students work in groups.

Suggested Responses:

Story element	Archetype	Symbolic significance in this story
Maypole	*Cosmic Tree*	*Central unifying emblem of the community*
Lord of the May	*vegetation god-king*	*Celebrated groom*
Lady of the May	*Goddess*	*Celebrated bride*
Rose leaves withering on Maypole	*Theme of death in life*	*Foreshadows the Puritan destruction of their ceremony and lifestyle*
Puritans	*Dark side of life*	*"Gloom"— sober virtues such as hard work, piety, sobriety*

4. Follow-up activity and/or homework: Ask students to write an essay on whether the maypole of this story is a sign, a symbol, and/or an archetype, referring to the earlier handouts in this unit if necessary. Indicate that they must provide a rationale for whichever definition they select.

5. Discuss with students the archetype of the sacred marriage as developed in this story. Ask them to consider the repercussions of this particular marriage: Is it an official ceremony even though it was performed outdoors instead of in a formal church or orthodox religious setting? Is it valid even though it was interrupted and spoiled by the Puritan band? What do students make of the ending? What does the author mean by "they went heavenward"? Do they die at the hands of the Puritans or is the couple incorporated into the Puritan society, showing that their true commitment transcends the situation they find themselves in in the world?

6. Bring in marriage relationships conveyed by other literature or poems studied during the year. This may lead into a discussion of the substance of marriage in general. Maybe ask students for their views on the subject: What signifies a true marriage? What makes the union? Is it the form or how the couple is wedded? Is it the ceremony and the subsequent lifestyle they choose? Or, is it the content of the relationship, the level of committment or the longevity of the marriage? Or, is it something else entirely?

7. Divide the class into two groups for a formal debate. One group will argue on behalf of the Merrymount colonists, and the other group will argue on behalf of the Puritans. (Each group may want to coin a name for their side.) Give each group time to prepare arguments. Arrange desks so the two panels face each other and coordinate the debate or have a designated student coordinate it. Suggested topic: Should Merrymount colonists have the right to live and worship nature without being disrupted?

Sacred Marriage—"The Maypole of Merrymount"

Read "The Maypole of Merrymount" by Nathaniel Hawthorne and list the archetypes, their story elements, and their symbolic significance in the story. One example is included.

Story element	Archetype	Symbolic significance in this story
Maypole	Cosmic Tree	Central unifying emblem of the community

Lesson 11
The Trickster

Objectives

- To introduce the trickster archetype

- To research and summarize myths featuring trickster characters

- To analyze the nature of this archetype and its function in our society

Notes to the Teacher

The trickster archetype is found in most cultural traditions throughout the world. It is depicted by different names and various personality types but includes several consistent features. The trickster has been described as being a wise-fool, an outrageous exhibitionist, a rascal who looks out for himself, as well as an inventive agent whose activities can benefit human society. This figure is usually male and appears in many stories as an animal full of craft and guile.

David Adam Leeming's *World of Myth* anthology has a section devoted to this character. Other secondary sources include the overview found in the *Encyclopedia of Religion*, volume 15, "trickster" entry. In this passage, scholar Laurence Sullivan points out the role of the trickster as a transformer and shaper of human culture—carnal, mocking, and duplicitous by nature. Sullivan sees in him "a symbol of the human condition" complete with sensual appetites and excesses, while his outrageousness acts as a foil to the more sublime character of the higher divinities. There are many other secondary sources which analyze the nature of this rascal. The classic study is Paul Radin's *Trickster: A Study in American Indian Mythology*, which includes Jung's own article entitled "On the Psychology of the Trickster-Figure" (This last article is also reproduced in Jung's *Four Archetypes*).

Students, having become competent at handling different archetypal figures, will be asked to discover for themselves examples of trickster figures in this lesson. It may be helpful to model one example with the class before they start on their independent research of the trickster character. Here is a list of some classic mythical trickster characters from world cultures to draw from (Examples of trickster tales can be found in the secondary sources cited in the Notes to the Teacher as well as in general anthologies of myths of the different cultural traditions listed):

Native American	Raven, Coyote, Blue Jay, Hare, Spider
Norse	Loki
Irish	Lugh
Polynesian (Hawaiian)	Maui
American South	Brer Rabbit
Indian	Krishna
Greek	Hermes
West Africa	Legba

A word of caution: Please note many of the tales deal with the tricksters' promiscuous nature and emphasize the lower animal functions and may not be appropriate for oral presentation or dramatization.

Procedure

1. Read two trickster myths aloud with students (See Notes to the Teacher for examples and sources). As a class, perhaps using a transparency, ask students to identify some obvious traits of this animal-archetype.

2. List possible archetypal trickster figures to be researched. Break students into small groups and have each group select an assignment. Instruct students to look into the myths and legends surrounding this character. Ask each group to write a summary description of this character and his or her mythic adventures to hand in to the teacher. Organize this into oral presentations or student produced skits (See caution in Notes to the Teacher!). In a class discussion, see if students can arrive at any lessons the trickster character imparts to the community; most will not be explicitly stated in the tales.

[1]*Encyclopedia of Religion*, s.v. "trickster."

3. Distribute **Handout 23**, part A the *Parabola* interview excerpt with Joseph Epes Brown, an authority on the Plains Indian lore, in which he discusses this trickster figure. Instruct students to read this article and answer the questions posed on part B of the handout. You may want students to work together on this activity.

Suggested Responses:

1. *A clown acts in a secular context; a trickster being acts in a religious context.*

2. *1. the element of shock; 2. communicate using humor*

3. *"Heyhoka" among the Sioux*

4. *Heyhoka=contrary. Answers will vary.*

5. *Vision experience involving certain forms and powers such as lightning*

6. *They shatter our everyday routine and force us to take a look at ourselves objectively.They remind us of the importance to laugh at ourselves.*

7. *Black Elk showed his people how to live spontaneously—"seizing the day"—by making his own fun. Also showed us religious spirituality can be experienced through laughter*

9. *Even though the shaman are performing "tricks" that people can see through, they are not considered "fake." Rather, it is looked at as an example of the illusory nature of life; everything in the world of appearances is illusion.*

10. *1. set parameters for acceptable behaviors; 2. instruct us in the shifting world of appearances as unreal; 3. entertain us; opens the door to deeper understanding of the world*

4. Lead a follow-up discussion assessment of the Trickster figure. Note the redeeming and/or incorrigible aspects of this figure. How does this figure rate against other archetypal figures studied in this unit? Is he a favorite with the students?

5. Possible evaluation activity: After reading the *Parabola* article and reviewing the responses to the handout questions, give students the following essay topics:

   1. How can the trickster be both a rascal and a hero figure to his people at the same time?

   2. What function does the trickster-Heyhoka figure serve for the tribe? Is there any comparable role in our society? Explain.

6. Optional Creative Activities:

   1. Ask students to write an interview with the trickster figure they researched in procedure 2, or another trickster figure they have come to favor. They may use the *Parabola* interview as a general model, but be sure they come up with original questions and responses for their trickster.

   2. Ask students to write an original myth or story placing their trickster figure as the central character. They may transfer the trickster's personality into human form if desired.

   3. Involve the entire class by presenting a "roast" in honor of one of the trickster figures. Have one student play the trickster being roasted and have the other members of the class compose testimonials to deliver regarding this character's mythological exploits.

The Wisdom of the Contrary
A Conversation with Joseph Epes Brown

Part A.

D.M. Dooling *We want to talk to you about the clown and the trickster who play such a prominent role in Native American cultures. In our culture we tend to think of him as being there for our entertainment: the circus or rodeo clown; something to amuse children. But perhaps even they have another, more hidden function. The rodeo clown, for instance: he isn't there simply to amuse the crowd with vulgar jokes; he's an extraordinarily brave man whose daring performances protect the riders from being trampled if they are thrown. But how could they be related, for example, to the Contraries of the Plains people?*

Joseph Epes Brown Before we get into details such as Contraries and the Plains people's traditions, would it be possible to talk a little bit about the meaning of the general phenomenon of "clowns" across cultures, and then come to specific references to American Indian cultures? I have some very strong feelings about this that I would like to verbalize, if I can. If you were to ask me to sit down and write about it, it would take me many weeks; informally, there are a few things I would like to speculate about.

D.D. *We would like very much to hear your speculations!*

J.B. I would like to emphasize first that we are here talking about "clowns," Contraries, or Trickster beings within essentially religious contexts—that is to say, within what I call traditional types of societies. When we talk about clowns in our society, such as the rodeo clown or the Barnum and Bailey circus clown, we are dealing with a different perspective, because here clowns and clowning occur outside a traditional religious context, although perhaps this is not so true in the origins of the circus. But today one could say that in our society—and this is perhaps not a kindly remark—clowns don't have the quality impact they do in traditional societies because it seems that in a society such as ours, everybody tends to be some kind of a clown, and life so often has the mood of a carnival, that the sacred context within which the traditional clown acts has become lost.

D.D. *Yes, it's not very kind, but rather true.*

J.B. Because with us, the carnival or the acts of a clown amuse but do not lead towards religious understanding or spiritual realization. In traditional societies in general, however, I would say that the role of the clown serves an enormously important purpose in that it opens a door, in a very subtle and effective way, into a realm of greater reality than the realm of the ebb and flow of everyday life. And this is accomplished, I think, essentially by two means. There is first of all the element of shock. Clowns among the Pueblos, for example, in the context of their ritual dance dramas, engage in, among other activities, sexual types of display which normally are quite taboo in such societies, and this causes a rupture with the ordinary everyday pattern of life. It does that by immediately catching the attention; it helps the people forget their petty little concerns about the routines of daily life. It shocks them out of that. Secondly, once that awareness, that alertness and openness, has been achieved through the initial shock, then it is possible to communicate on another level through the use of humor. As I see it, all this puts the mind of the person involved in a frame which relates to the humor of the situation, thus serving to open doors to a realm greater than that of ordinary life. It does this extremely effectively, because all of this takes place, as I have suggested, within a very serious ritual or dance-drama context, which involves enormous concentration, great attention to the minute details of the rites of the ceremonies that are being carried out—and the rigors of all this demand some kind of relief, some way in which what is being stated through the rites can be translated onto a much deeper level, transcending the activities, or the forms and motions of the rite itself. Thus shock and humor open into another realm. It is a very Zen-like technique, it seems to me.

D.D. *Yes, I was just thinking of the traditional Zen master, who certainly uses the technique of shock and humor. But I have a question there: the humor is apparently very often directed toward the rite itself. It's as if the ritual solemnities were being made fun of. Now from what you say, I gather that you think this is done in order that the truth that is within these rites should be somehow put on a different level, but not destroyed; would you say the humor is not destructive, it is not* against?

J.B. No, I see it as a technique to translate the formal rite or to break through it into an area of deeper meaning and deeper awareness on the part of the participant. It is you might say a shattering of the structure of the rite in order to get at the essence of the rite. It seems to ridicule, thus destroy, but it does this so that deeper truths contained within the rite can come forth and reveal themselves.

D.D. *I wonder if you could describe some manifestations of the trickster or the clown when this role is being played?*

J.B. Well, there are many examples one could take, but I always like to use those out of Plains Indian culture, out of my own experience with the so-called *Heyhokas* among the Sioux, especially among the friends I lived with in Black Elk's family, and with Black Elk himself, who was a *Heyhoka*—

D.D. *He was? I didn't know that!*

J.B. Oh, yes! In the first place, to become a *Heyhoka*, or sometimes what is called a Contrary, requires a deep spiritual experience—a very intense quality of dream, or more often a vision experience. This sacred origin is important, because it gives the key to the fact that what we are really dealing with in the activities of the *Heyhoka* is of a spiritual nature, and is a means of transmitting spiritual truths to the larger community. The quality of the vision that leads to becoming a *Heyhoka* is institutionalized in a sense, in that it has to be a vision involving certain forms or certain powers—lightning, for example, the Thunder Beings, or the dog; if one has such a vision, this requires that the person becomes a *Heyhoka*.

D.D. *Any vision of any one of these?*

J.B. At least among the Sioux, yes. However, the strongest sign probably is of lightning, whether in the form of the Thunder Beings, or the eagle perhaps, which is associated with lightning. This was Black Elk's experience, which forced him to become a trickster figure, a *Heyhoka*, one who has the obligation—and it is a very weighty function that is imposed on such a person—to do things in ways which break with the traditional norms. Sometimes the *Heyhoka's* actions are very humorous, because this is, as we have said, a part of the technique for shattering a person's perception of, and participation in, the everyday routines of life. To break through the habitual enables one to take some distance from oneself—to see things a little bit more objectively, and thereby on a higher level. So the *Heyhokas* do all sorts of strange things: they do things upside down or backwards; sometimes they will pitch a tepee with the poles on the outside of the lodge covering, with the smoke flaps facing the wrong way, or with the doorway to the west instead of to the east. When they sit in the tepee maybe they will do it upside down, with their feet up in the air, lying on their backs on the ground; and this of course makes people laugh. Normally when you enter a tepee in the Plains, you must move around it in a sunwise direction, clockwise; but the *Heyhoka* will do it the wrong way. Everything is done in reverse. Sometimes instead of going in the doorway they lift up the lodge cover at the back and crawl under; things like that. Sometimes their tricks aren't so funny. I remember one story an old Sioux woman told me, and she was really mad about it. Her husband was a *Heyhoka*, and she had just finished making a pair of decorated moccasins for him. They were in the lodge and she tossed them to him across the fire, saying, "Here, try them on." In their language, which is Lakota, that sounds very much like, "Here, burn them up," and so he picked them up and threw them into the fire, and burned up his nice new moccasins; and she was very furious. She didn't think that was very funny.

D.D.   *I really can't blame her!*

J.B.   But maybe it did something for her, to help her to take a greater distance from her craft work. Sometimes in making things one becomes too attached to what is made, forgetting that things are never permanent!

There are hundreds of stories like that. I like the one Black Elk used to tell about the *Heyhokas* who rushed out of the tepee after a little sprinkle of rain and saw a large puddle; with great flourishes and gesticulations they took off their clothes down to the breech clout, and then they got a long pole, about twenty feet long, and laid it horizontally across the puddle; then they set it up vertically in order to measure the depth of the water, and saw it was about twenty feet deep, you see? So with a great deal of display, making sure everybody in camp was looking, they dove into the water, which was only a few inches deep, and hit their heads hard, and made everybody laugh. And that's good, because what is life without laughter? It's very important.

D.D.   *What did Black Elk do as a* Heyhoka?

J.B.   Well, he was always doing funny things. That it why it was always good to live with him, because you never knew what to expect. It was always something completely unexpected that would happen, when you were traveling with him, for instance. There was a time—this isn't exactly humorous, but it shows the ability of the *Heyhoka* to seize on any occasion and use it in an imaginative, unusual way. It was in Denver—which was not a very pleasant city in the early 1940s; there was a great deal of prejudice and racism, and we had a hard time finding a hotel room. When we did find one it was a very dingy, horrible room and Black Elk felt bad about Denver and the hotel; he felt unclean and he wanted a sweat bath to cleanse himself of the impurities of that city. I didn't know how this could be done in a hotel room; but the room was heated by a coal fire, and the fireplace was brick and so old the bricks were falling out of it. He said, "Here, let's take there loose bricks, and we'll pull some more out of the chimney and heat them in the coal fire," which we did. Then we took the chairs in the room and put them in a circle, and took all the bedding off the beds and put them over the chairs to make a kind of lodge right there in the middle of this hotel room. We found an old coal scuttle and when the bricks were red hot we put them in the coal scuttle, put that in the little lodge, and stripped down and crawled in; and it was good and hot in there and we sang and prayed and smoked and sweated and it was real good, you know? I think that was the first time a sweat bath has ever been taken in a Denver hotel room; but that is typical of the kind of thing that happens with these people—the unexpected, breaking with habitual patterns, adds a dimension to life that I think is terribly important.

D.D.   *When Black Elk was acting as a religious leader among his people, did he put aside the* Heyhoka *role?*

J.B.   No; it is incumbent upon the *Heyhoka* always to be a *Heyhoka*; you can't turn it on and off.

D.D.   *How did he reconcile the two roles?*

J.B.   The leading of serious, sacred rites isn't contrary to breaking the seriousness of those rites with humor. It gives dramatic relief; it is a universal technique. Very often, right in the middle of a sacred rite, the opening of a medicine bundle, for instance, there'll be a kind of break or recess, and at that time maybe they'll start telling very funny stories; and in this most serious context all of a sudden everyone is laughing and rolling around on the ground.

D.D. *That reminds me of an experience of my own, when I was admitted to the preparation of a Navajo sand painting ceremony. At the same time that the medicine man was making the sand painting, and instructing a couple of young assistants in exactly how it was done, he was also making great fun of us, and there was a great deal of laughter. They would stop every now and then and say, "Thankyou thankyou thankyou!" They think it is very funny the way we say "thank you," and the laughter was uproarious. It was my first experience of Native Americans in action and I was very much astonished at this mixture of the solemn with ridicule.*

J.B. And so often for an outsider it is very, very hard to take, because we feel offended, and so on. But if we really stand off from ourselves and see that indeed we really *are* very funny in certain circumstances, and start to laugh at ourselves, then all of a sudden—and this I think is the point of the whole thing—something opens up and another quality of participation becomes possible. You know, in many of those cults or sects where everything is taken so very seriously and everything must be very solemn and one must never smile because a smile is against religion, one wonders—in a truly spiritual sense, what is the real work that goes on within? In many American Indian cultures, on the Northwest coast, for instance, certain rites and ceremonies can't be started until the guests who have been invited to participate start to laugh—open up. Once they start to laugh, then the ground is prepared for a real quality of participation in the sacred dimensions of what the rite is all about.

. . . .

There is something that I think is very important about these kinds of tricks and strange phenomena that some of the medicine men can accomplish: very often it is evident to the outsider that there is some pragmatic explanation for the trick, some sleight of hand or other, and very often that is the case and the people are very aware of it. But that doesn't mean to them that the performer is a fake or a charlatan; they relate to this in a different kind of way from the way we would—not with suspicion but with an understanding that however the phenomenon was accomplished, it illustrates the illusory nature of phenomena in general. And realizing the illusory nature of phenomena, the world of appearances, of *maya* as the Hindus would say, again helps one to break through to a reality that is more real.

D.D. *Do you remember an article of Sam Gill's, in an early issue of* Parabola, *in which he was speaking of just that among the Hopi, with the kachinas? There is a disillusionment of the children at a certain age: they have been brought up with all sorts of Santa Claus stories about the kachinas. He also spoke about some tribes in Australia and the initiation rites for young boys, where they frighten them to death with bullroarers, keeping them blindfolded, and then suddenly the blindfolds are taken off and they see that these terrible roaring gods are their own fathers, laughing at them! He made a very interesting case for the extraordinary effect that this could have on the children, of bringing them to an entirely different level of understanding.*

J.B. Right—that is what I feel is accomplished. He was writing about the kachina initiation rites of the Hopi and how after very serious rites, indeed, a terrifying display where the initiates are whipped, all of a sudden the elders take off their masks and start whipping each other and joking and the children see they are their fathers and uncles and so on. So you have again the theme of the shock and then release of tension with humor, and then hopefully understanding on a deeper level which is appropriate at this particular age; they are old enough now to understand the mysteries of the kachinas, but on a deeper level possible with maturity.

D.D. *I don't succeed in understanding very well the connection here with the enormous body of Trickster myths—all the shenanigans of Coyote, for instance, combined with his semi-divinity. What is the intention there?*

J.B. Yes, these tales now involve not people who take on the role of the clown, but animal or mythical beings who take on similar functions, whether it is Coyote, the Algonkin Nanabozo, the Great Hare, or the Siouan *Iktomi*, the Spider. First of all, the stories are always transmitted orally by storytellers, the elders who are often great artists, actors who are able to tell it in a way that immediately catches the attention of the children, the old people, everybody. They use all kinds of dramatic devices to hold their listeners' attention. Also the telling of these tales is always under certain circumstances: sometimes only in the winter season, as among the Navajos, after certain beings have gone underground, like bears and spiders, who have negative potentialities. Or, in addition, they may only be told at nighttime; in other words, the context in which the tales are told has to be special, and that lends importance to the telling of them. Then the tales themselves are acted out, often using many theatrical devices, and most of them present things that one isn't supposed to do in everyday life—as in the Coyote tales. For example, Coyote is always complaining about his hunger; and everybody knows you should never do that. So when the moment comes when he complains of hunger, everybody laughs, because they know this is not appropriate. Or Coyote is always being carried away by his sex impulses, and again everybody laughs because they know that such excesses are not acceptable behavior. Of course eventually Coyote gets punished for allowing his appetites to run away with him; but a number of things happen in these tales on a number of different levels. First of all there is what you might call the moralistic level. (There is never the punch line that we have in Aesop's fables: "This is what happens if you do this"—everybody gets the point without having to emphasize it like that.) On this moralistic level, the tales set the parameters for acceptable behavior; they define the limits outside of which you are not allowed to go if you are a member of that particular cultural group. Secondly, on what seems to me a higher level of understanding, the miraculous events that are always a part of the tale instruct us that this shifting world of appearances is not really real; there are other levels of reality. For instance, Coyote is tricked into a hollow log and can't get out, nevertheless he is able to take a clamshell from behind his ear and he cuts the parts of his body into tiny pieces and throws them out of a knothole; then once outside he puts himself together again. Thus these episodes again help to break the shell of this world of appearances in which we tend to be too set. Then there is the humor, too, and these together, as with the clown, open up the possibility of participation on other, deeper levels of reality. It is a *most* effective device, whether used by the clown or in the adventures of the Trickster being.

D.D. *Are there special people who are allowed to tell stories? Do they tell them in their houses, or is there a communal storytelling? Or does this vary?*

J.B. It varies a great deal. Sometimes just in the evening when the family is there, an elder is chosen, or spontaneously he begins to tell the story, or it may be a younger person who is noted for his skill in using dramatic devices. Such oral transmission is a great art form, and it is a tragedy that this has been disappearing over the past years. With the emphasis on literacy and so on it has been increasingly lost to the people, with all that this implies. For these truths are the kinds of things that are transmitted only through the oral traditions. Also, for the full import of the tales they must be told in their own language.

Part B.

Analyzing the Trickster

Read the *Parabola* magazine article "The Wisdom of the Contrary, A conversation with Joseph Epes Brown," **Handout 23,** part A, and answer the following questions:

1. What is the difference between a clown and a trickster?

2. Identify the two ways a clown in a traditional society opens the door to a greater reality than the everyday flow. Explain how each is accomplished.

3. What term do the native American Plains Indians give to this figure?

4. What images does the translation of that term call to mind? Is it a descriptive term to use in this case? Using the examples of trickster figures you've already researched for this lesson, explain why or why not.

5. What sign is taken in the Sioux tribe as an indication that one is a trickster figure?

6. What lessons can we learn from this character according to the Joseph Epes Brown interview?

7. How does a tribal leader like Black Elk manage his trickster personality to benefit his people?

8. Why is it important to laugh at ourselves?

9. What is the message behind the "tricks" and sleight of hand that the trickster is performing?

10. What are the three functions behind the trickster tales? Are any of these devices used by contemporary comic characters in addressing their audience? Explain.

11. How do stories get told in your family?

Lesson 12
The Scapegoat

Objectives
• To introduce the archetypal figure of the scapegoat

• To analyze this archetype in the context of a short story and our own culture

Notes to the Teacher
The scapegoat is the final archetypal figure covered in this unit. As the title suggests, this character assumes the blame for the plight which is afflicting society. In each instance, the scapegoat pays a terrible price to rectify these social ills. For different reasons—sometimes a tragic flaw, sometimes poor judgment, sometimes for simply having the bad luck to be in the wrong place at the wrong time—the person assigned the role of scapegoat must be sacrificed. They are forced to give their lives to atone for the accumulated sins of their society, thereby restoring normal order and equilibrium to it.

The scapegoat character in myth, drama, and literature is a social phenomenon. David Adams Lemming touches upon this motif in *World of Myth,* discussing the rebirth process in the dying god archetype citing the Biblical reference: "Since the goat is to carry off their iniquities to an isolated region, it must be sent away into the desert." (Leviticus 16:22) Sir James Frazer's classic multi-volume study *The Golden Bough* considers this theme in depth. Scholar Eliade notes a parallel between this scapegoat motif and the idea behind ceremonial sacrifices known as "first-fruits" in *Patterns in Comparative Religion.* He writes of these as purification offerings made by primitive people in agricultural societies to appease their anxieties over the "power" they saw operating in the seasonal cycles of nature, especially during harvest-time. Eliade believes these sacrifices "were offered to reconcile mankind with the forces at work in them and to obtain permission for mankind to use them without danger."[1] These primitive rituals were made to ensure the regeneration of the natural order and the community itself.

The haunting short story by Shirley Jackson, "The Lottery," is the basis for this lesson and may be used as a directed reading activity. (Or, if students are capable, as an independent reading assignment, with follow-up teacher facilitated discussions.) There is a film version of "The Lottery" designated under *The Short-story Showcase* series, by Encyclopedia Brittanica Educational Corp.,1969 (28 minutes) (OCLC #11594102).

Procedure
1. Begin the lesson by indicating several tragic hero figures that the students have studied or become familiar with in literature and myth (Osiris, Dionysis, Hamlet, Oedipus, Othello, or Hedda Gabler) and note some commonality between these figures.

2. Explain the fundamentals of "a lottery" as background if necessary, indicating that there is a definite distinction between the various state run "jackpot" lotteries and the one portrayed in this story.

3. Ask students to read "The Lottery." Inform students that this story is the product of writer Shirley Jackson's imagination and it was written during the mid 1940s during her residence in North Bennington, Vermont. Share the following anecdote: Jackson got the idea for this story while wheeling her young children up the hill in their stroller coming home from a trip to the little village one day. When she got home, she managed to get the story down in writing while it was fresh in her mind. At the time it was published, she received a *tremendous* volume of mail inquiring into the origin and factual basis of the story. Assure students that we have the author's word that it is a *fictional* account of the scapegoat scenario.

---

[1] Mircea Eliade, *Patterns in Comparative Religion* (Kansas City: Sheed and Ward Inc., 1958), 346–347.

4. Discuss students' impressions of the story. Touch upon the inherent irony and the symbolic meaning. Decide what the author is trying to uncover about human nature and social order.

5. Distribute **Handout 24** and have students answer the questions for comprehension and/or review.

Suggested Responses:

1. *The ritual may reflect the third of Campbell's functions covering the sociological dimension; it defines the individuals in the society, singling out one to act as the scapegoat and structures their behavior in this situation. To a lesser extent, it may also reflect function two as it annually restores the community's order. The reason why they continue with this ritual is not explicitly evident in the text. Speculation may include the folk-wisdom expressed by Old Man Warner, "Lottery in June, corn be soon," as a link between the human sacrifice and the reaping of the harvest. (Students may hear echos in this expression of the vegetation god having to be sacrificed to ensure the earth's fertility.) Old Man Warner indicates that if they discontinued the Lottery, there would be no crop to harvest and the people would have to subsist by foraging for wild foods.*

2. *She comes across as animated and a little scatterbrained. She seems to be in a light-hearted mood, jesting, etc. This is a contrast to the gravity of the situation. Mrs. Delacroix conveys a friendliness toward her in the first encounter, yet at the end she picks up a huge rock to stone her.*

3. *Mr. Summers is all business as he formally conducts the Lottery, but he also manages things in a friendly manner. His name signifies the time of year, the height of summer, June 27. This is known as midsummer, just after the summer solstice when everything is green and blooming. This time of nature flourishing is a direct contrast to the objective of the Lottery, to single out a community member to put to death by stoning.*

4. *Perhaps people used to accept the results of the Lottery with a more submissive attitude rather than challenging it.*

5. *Mrs. Hutchinson acts in an understandable self-preservation mode, ranting about the unfairness of the result.*

5. Using this story and students' other experiences with reading about tragic figures arrive at a class definition of scapegoat. (Possibly, bring in the Biblical origin of the term from Leviticus 16:20–28.) Ask students to reflect upon the concept of atonement as it is achieved in this story as opposed to the way it is approached through the legal system in our culture. Are there any similarities between the two systems? Does our so-called civilized approach to reconciling wrongs and making reparation work?

6. Follow-up activity and/or homework assignment: Involve students in brainstorming some examples of scapegoat figures in our own society. Examples may include unfortunate figures who have been cast into this role due to their political, prisoner and/or minority status. Consider what purpose these figures serve for society.

Name_____

Date_____

"The Lottery"

Read "The Lottery" by Shirley Jackson and answer the following questions:

1. Evaluate the ritual of the lottery. Does it correspond with any of Campbell's four functions covered in Lesson 3? Why does this town feel obligated to continue the tradition?

2. What is Mrs. Hutchinson's demeanor as she joins the assembly? Note the discrepancy between Mrs. Delacroix's attitude toward her at this point and at the end of the story.

3. Describe the character of Mr. Summers. What is his role in the proceedings? Think about the irony of his name and the setting the author chooses as a backdrop for the story. Consider especially the significance of the time of year.

4. What is the implication behind Old Man Warner's remark, "It's not the way it used to be. People ain't the way they used to be," as the Hutchinson's make the final draw?

5. What is Mrs. Hutchinson's demeanor at the end of the story? Does this character evoke your sympathy, or righteousness, or any other emotion?

Additional Activities and Projects

1. Send students to the local art museum, if one is available. Also have them look into art history textual references to view examples of archetypes (especially the Great Mother Goddess) as depicted in the visual arts, painting, sculpture, etc. Encourage students to discover the power of these symbolic forms for themselves. Follow-up with a reflection paper discussing these representations.

2. Have students attend a live performance of music, dance, or drama if possible. Have them identify the archetypal themes and/or characters being presented. Follow-up with a reflection paper on this experience.

3. Have students design representations of archetypal figures using the medium of visual arts and/ or performing arts. Examples may include making masks, writing skits, or producing paintings or murals of their favorite archetypal characters.

4. Have students view and write reviews of films and documentaries which illustrate archetypal themes. For example, *Apollo 13* illustrates the archetype of flight; and *An American Quilt* illustrates several archetypes including the benevolent guide and liberation of transcendence. Have them indicate any symbolic representation the filmmaker uses to convey his or her vision.

5. Have students put together a musical presentation of these archetypal themes using a favorite type of music, such as folk or classical. They should indicate the symbolic significance of the music by discussing the lyrics and/or other musical structures used by the composer to convey his or her vision.

6. Have students explore other mediums of popular culture, such as comic books, pop art, and fashion statements which suggest archetypal themes.

Some Suggestions for Supplementary Reading:

Mother Archetype	*Light in August*, William Faulkner
	To The Lighthouse, Virginia Woolf
	Greenleaf, Flannery O'Connor
Female Initiation	*The Woman Warrior*, Maxine Hong Kingston
	North to the Orient, Anne Morrow Lindbergh
Male Initiation	*Moby Dick*, Herman Melville
	Huckleberry Finn, Mark Twain
	Wind, Sand and Stars, Antoine De Saint-Exupery
Benevolent Guide	*The Once and Future King*, T.H. White
Sacred Marriage	*The Dubliners*, James Joyce
Trickster	*The Cocktail Party*, T.S. Eliot
Scapegoat	*Lord of the Flies*, William Golding

Suggestions for Timed-Essay Practice Using the *Archetypes in Life, Literature, and Myth* Unit

1. Select a prose passage illustrating one of the archetypes you have encountered in this unit. Write an essay in which you describe the author's use of the archetype as a dynamic symbol.

2. The archetype of initiation is a standard theme in literary works. Select one work which reflects this theme and write a well-organized essay which illustrates the way the author weaves the story around it.

3. Select a poem you have studied in this unit to show how the archetypal theme of birth-death-rebirth is delivered by the poet. Include descriptive imagery and analysis in your essay.

4. Select a mythic motif which illustrates how an archetypal figure functions in a social setting. Include an analysis of this figure and its effect on the society at large in your organized essay.

5. In a well-organized essay, describe a mythical, fairytale, or folk hero or heroine's adventure quest in terms of the type of intitation he or she elects to undertake. Include all the features of whichever initiation is being experienced by the protagonist: monomyth or liberation of transcendence.

6. Write an account of a revelation (epiphany*) experienced by a character from a story featuring an initiation theme. Describe the importance of this experience to the plot in a well-organized essay.

7. Take a substantial figure or issue from current-events and discuss it in terms of its symbolic and/or archetypal significance. Indicate the function of this phenomenon for an individual and/or society. Write an organized essay incorporating the elements discussed in this unit.

8. Select one archetypal figure encountered in this unit and show how it manifests itself differently according to its context. For example, explore the difference between a wise-fool character as it appears in a Shakespearean play vs. tribal account of a mythical trickster-god vs. a modern-day comedian. Include the similarities between the manifestations of the archetype in your essay.

9. Select one of the archetypes or archetypal patterns discussed in this unit and write a well-organized essay in which you articulate its significance to you personally. Discuss its function and describe the importance it holds for you at this point in your life.

Note: These are not to be plot summaries of the story or myth. Your instructor will set a time limit (set between thirty and forty minutes).

The literary term epiphany refers to a sudden insight into life which is sometimes granted to an artist. This term was applied by James Joyce to his collection of short stories, The Dubliners.

Bibliography

Bettelheim, Bruno. *The Uses of Enchantment: The Meaning and Importance of Fairytales.* New York: Random House Vintage Books Ed., 1977.

Burland, CA. *Myths of Life and Death.* New York: Crown Publishers Inc., 1974.

Campbell, Joseph. *The Hero with a Thousand Faces.* Princeton N.J.: Princeton University Press, 1977.

_____. *Masks of God, Volume 3, Occidental Mythology.* New York: Penguin Books, 1976.

_____, ed. *Myths, Dreams and Religion.* Society for the Arts, Religion, Continuing Culture Inc. 1970.

_____. *Myths to Live By.* New York: Viking Press, 1972.

_____. *The Power of Myth* New York: Doubleday, 1988.

Carlyon, Richard. *A Guide to the Gods.* Great Britain: William Heinemann, 1981.

Colum, Padraic. *Myths of the World.* New York: Universal Library Grosset and Dunlap, 1930.

Doniger O'Flaherty, Wendy. *Other People's Myths: The Cave of Echos,* New York: Macmillan, 1988.

Eliade, Mircea. *The Quest, History and Meaning in Religion.* Chicago: University of Chicago Press, 1969.

_____. *Patterns in Comparative Religion.* Kansas City: Streed and Ward Inc., 1958.

_____. *Rites and Symbols of Initiation: The Mysteries of Birth and Rebirth.* New York: Harper and Row, 1965.

_____. *Symbolism, the Sacred & the Arts.* New York: Crossroad Pub. Co., 1985.

Estes, Clarissa Pinkola. *Women Who Run with the Wolves: Myths and Stories of the Wild Woman Archetype.* New York: Ballantine Books, 1992.

Gadon, Elinor. *The Once and Future Goddess: A Sweeping Visual Chronicle of the Sacred Female and Her Reemergence in the Cultural Mythology of Our Time.* New York: Harper & Row, 1989.

Grant, Michael. *Myths of the Greeks and Romans.* New York: The New American Library, 1962.

Hall, T. William, Richard B. Pilgrim and Ronald R. Cavanagh. *Religion: An Introduction.* New York: Harper, 1986.

Harding, Esther M. *Woman's Mysteries Ancient and Modern.* New York: HarperCollins Books, 1971.

Henderson, Joseph and Oakes, Maud. *The Wisdom of the Serpent: The Myths of Death, Rebirth and Resurrection.* New York: George Braziller, Inc, 1963.

Jung, C.G. *Four Archetypes: Mother/Rebirth/Spirit/Trickster.* Princeton: Princeton University Press, 1969.

_____, ed. *Man and His Symbols.* New York: Doubleday, Aldus Books, 1964.

Larsen, Stephen. *The Shaman's Doorway,* New York: Harper & Row, 1976.

Leeming, David Adams. *The World of Myth: An Anthology,* New York: Oxford University Press, 1990.

Lincoln, Bruce. *Emerging from the Chrysalis: Studies in Rituals of Women's Initiation,* Cambridge: Harvard University Press, 1981.

Martin, P.W. *Experiment in Depth.* London: Routledge & Kegan Paul Ltd., 1955.

Neumann, Erich (trans. Ralph Manheim). *The Great Mother: An Analysis of the Archetype.* Princeton: Princeton University Press, 1974.

Schmidt, Roger. *Exploring Religion.* Belmont,CA: Wadsworth Pub.Co., 1988.

Smith, Huston. *The World's Religions: Our Great Wisdom Traditions.* New York: Harper Collins, 1991.

Woolger, Jennifer Barker and Roger. *The Goddess Within: A Guide to Eternal Myths that Shape Women's Lives,* New York: Fawcett Columbine, 1989.

Videos

"The Lottery" by Shirley Jackson. *The Short Story Showcase Series.* Encyclopedia Brittanica Corporation, 1969 (28 minutes). OCLC #11594102

"The Power of Myth" Joseph Campbell and Bill Moyer six-part television series on videocassettes. Mystic Fire Video, P.O. Box 30969, Dept. DL, New York, NY 10011; or call 1–800–727–8433.

Acknowledgments

For permission to reprint all works in this volume, grateful acknowledgment is made to the following holders of copyright, publisher, or representatives.

Lesson 1, Procedure

For use of definitions of archetype and symbol, from *The Continuum Dictionary of Religion*, Michael Pye, editor. Copyright © 1994, Macmillan Press Limited, New York.

Lesson 1, Handouts 1, 2
Lesson 2, Procedures
Lesson 7, Notes to the Teacher
Lesson 10, Notes to the Teacher

For use of excerpts, pages 20-21 from *Man and His Symbols* by C.G. Jung. Definition of archetypes also adapted from *Man and His Symbols*, pages 63–107. Copyright © 1964. Used with permission from J.G. Ferguson Co., Chicago, Illinois.

Lesson 2, Handout 5

"Of Walt Whitman, Who Could Hear America Singing," by Paul Greenberg. Found in *The Plain Dealer*, July 5, 1995, page 12B. Used with acknowledgment to Los Angeles Times Syndicate, Los Angeles, California.

Lesson 3, Handout 8

"Birth of the Bomb," found in *The News Herald*, July 16, 1995, pages A2 and A26. Used with acknowledgment to Fred Bruning, copyright holder and author, Mentor, Ohio.

Lesson 3, Handout 9

"Disney's version of Pocahantas unlike the historical" by Joan Connell. Found in *The Plain Dealer*, June 27, 1995, page 6E. Used with acknowledgment to Religion News Service, New York.

Lesson 4, Notes to the Teacher

For use of charts from *The Goddess Within* by Roger and Jennifer Barker Woolger. Copyright © 1987, Ballantine Books, New York, a division of Random House.

Lesson 8, Handout 18

"Departure" by Edna St. Vincent Millay. From *Collected Poems*, HarperCollins. Copyright 1923, 1951 by Edna St. Vincent Millay and Norma Millay Ellis. Reprinted by permission of Elizabeth Barnett, Literary Executor.

Lesson 11, Notes to the Teacher

Citation: From "Tricksters: An Overview" by Lawrence E. Sullivan, in *The Encyclopedia of Religion*, Mircea Eliade, Editor in Chief. Vol. 15, pp. 45–46. Copyright © 1987 by Macmillan Publishing Company. Used by permission of Macmillan Reference USA, a Division of Simon & Schuster.

Lesson 11, Handout 23

For use of "The Wisdom of the Contrary: A Conversation with Joseph Epes Brown." Found in *Parabola Magazine*, a Tamarack Press Publication. Vol. 4, No. 1, Feb. 1979.

Lesson 12, Notes to the Teacher

Scripture texts are taken from *The New American Bible with Revised New Testament* copyright © 1991 by the Confraternity of Christian Doctrine, Washington, D.C. 20017 and are used with permission. All rights reserved.

Language Arts Series

Advanced Placement

Advanced Placement English: Practical Approaches to Literary Analysis
Advanced Placement English: In-depth Analysis of Literary Forms
Advanced Placement Poetry
Advanced Placement Short Story
Advanced Placement Writing 1
Advanced Placement Writing 2

Composition

Advanced Composition
Basic Composition
Creative Writing
Daily Writing Topics
Formula Writing 1—Building Toward Writing Proficiency
Formula Writing 2—Diverse Writing Situations
Grammar Mastery—For Better Writing, Workbook Level 1
Grammar Mastery—For Better Writing, Workbook Level 2
Grammar Mastery—For Better Writing, Teacher Guide
Journalism: Writing for Publication
Research 1: Information Literacy
Research 2: The Research Paper
Writing 1: Learning the Process
Writing 2: Personalizing the Process
Writing Short Stories
Writing Skills and the Job Search

Genres

Mythology
Nonfiction: A Critical Approach
Participating in the Poem
Science Fiction—19th Century
Short Poems: Their Vitality and Versatility
The Short Story

Literary Traditions

American Literature 1: Beginnings through Civil War
American Literature 2: Civil War to Present
Archetypes in Life, Literature, and Myth
British Literature 1: Beginnings to Age of Reason
British Literature 2: Romantics to the Present
Honors American Literature 1
Honors American Literature 2
Multicultural Literature: Essays, Fiction, and Poetry
World Literature 1
World Literature 2

Skills

Creative Dramatics in the Classroom
Junior High Language Arts
Speech
Thinking, Reading, Writing, Speaking

Special Topics

Supervisor/Student Teacher Manual
Peer Mediation: Training Students in Conflict Resolution

The Publisher

All instructional materials identified by the TAP® (Teachers/ Authors/Publishers) trademark are developed by a national network of teachers whose collective educational experience distinguishes the publishing objective of The Center for Learning, a non-profit educational corporation founded in 1970.

Concentrating on values-related disciplines, the Center publishes humanities and religion curriculum units for use in public and private schools and other educational settings. Approximately 500 language arts, social studies, novel/drama, life issues, and faith publications are available.

While acutely aware of the challenges and uncertain solutions to growing educational problems, the Center is committed to quality curriculum development and to the expansion of learning opportunities for all students. Publications are regularly evaluated and updated to meet the changing and diverse needs of teachers and students. Teachers may offer suggestions for development of new publications or revisions of existing titles by contacting

The Center for Learning

Administrative/Editorial Office
21590 Center Ridge Road
Rocky River, OH 44116
(440) 331-1404 • FAX (440) 331-5414
E-mail: cfl@stratos.net
Web: www.centerforlearning.org

For a free catalog, containing order and price information, and a descriptive listing of titles, contact

The Center for Learning

Shipping/Business Office
P.O. Box 910
Villa Maria, PA 16155
(724) 964-8083 • (800) 767-9090
FAX (888) 767-8080